W9-CCR-603

Professionalism
and
Pastoral Care

THEOLOGY AND PASTORAL CARE SERIES

edited by
Don S. Browning

ALASTAIR V. CAMPBELL

Professionalism and Pastoral Care

Don S. Browning, *editor*

THEOLOGY AND PASTORAL CARE

FORTRESS PRESS
PHILADELPHIA

Library of Congress Cataloging in Publication Data

Campbell, Alastair V.

Professionalism and pastoral care.

(Theology and pastoral care series)
Bibliography: p.
1. Pastoral theology. 2. Clergy—Office.
3. Professions. I. Title. II. Series.
BV4011.4.C36 1985   253   84-48710
ISBN 0-8006-1733-9

1264K84   Printed in the United States of America   1-1733

Contents

70969

Series Foreword

Alastair Campbell is no stranger to the American church community. His contributions to the literature on pastoral care already have established him as one of the leading writers on subjects related to the care dimensions of ministry. The vantage point of his observations and experience add special power to his message. Alastair Campbell teaches in the Department of Christian Ethics and Practical Theology at the University of Edinburgh. He is the author of the widely appreciated *Rediscovering Pastoral Care.*

Although Professor Campbell teaches in Scotland, he is deeply knowledgeable about the literature on and experience of ministry in the United States. In fact, he is an extremely astute observer of the situation of the church and ministry in both of these parts of the world. Hence, Campbell brings a comparative perspective to his comments on professionalism and pastoral care that makes his book alive with sparkling insights about the nature of ministry in the modern world.

Professor Campbell has read widely in the literature on the history and contemporary expressions of professionalism. He understands how various models and theories of professionalism have influenced present-day forms of ministry. This is especially true in the care and counseling aspects of ministry. More than we sometimes admit, the specialized forms of professional secular counseling and psychotherapy have shaped the way we think not only about pastoral care and counseling but about the nature of ordained ministry as a whole. Campbell is aware of how deeply the pastoral care and counseling movements in the United States have absorbed the ethos and self-understanding of the specialized secular helping professions. Although this trend is more advanced in the United States, Campbell understands the extent to which similar developments have begun to take place in Scotland and England and asks whether the encroachment of these professional models of ministry should be resisted and reversed.

Campbell is not so much antiprofessional as he is desirous of locating the professional role of ordained minister in its proper place within the total ministry of the church. Campbell is clearly afraid of the inequality, intellectualism, and individualism that the professional model can inject into the life of the church. In order to avoid these excesses, professionalism must be balanced with an appropriate emphasis on the care of the whole church, the laity as well as the ordained minister. To balance intellectualism and its related emphasis upon theory, there must be a renewed emphasis upon story and simple human presence. In contrast to the specialization and individualism of professionalism, there must be an emphasis upon pastoral care as the building up of the Christian community as a whole and the ministry of this community to the world beyond itself.

Alastair Campbell has been profoundly influenced by the earlier writings of R. A. Lambourne, an English pastoral theologian whose writings in the early 1960s played a substantial role in heading off the rush toward professionalization of ministry in England and Scotland. Although Campbell is not a reactionary and does not advocate dispensing with the positive aspects of a professional model, this book goes far in restoring an image of pastoral care that retains yet balances recent specialized and clergy-dominated images of the church's ministries of care and counseling. Campbell's own pastoral touch, and the remarkable case histories that he uses so liberally to illustrate his points, make this book a treasure for increasing our understanding of the care and counseling ministries of the church.

Don S. Browning

Introduction

This book—perhaps more than most—is a product of the author's own uncertainty. I find the idea that pastoral care should be regarded as a professional activity both attractive and unacceptable. There is an obvious attraction in the competence, consistency, and dedication of the professional person. These qualities certainly enhance any form of caring. Yet, at the same time, the claim to competence and to acknowledged authority seems to accord very badly with the theological insight that we all fall short of the love that God both offers to us and requires of us. Do we really dare to lay claim to an expertise in Christian love? The pages that follow spell out the implications of this critical question. The reader must judge whether this leads to greater clarification or merely to the sharing of uncertainty, but, in any event, I have tried to pursue the argument as specifically and practically as possible. I hope that the issues I have raised will be of direct relevance to all who attempt to offer pastoral care, whether or not they have any recognized office in the church, for this is intended to be a book for all who hope to honor the command to love both God and neighbor.

I wish to express my thanks to Don Browning, the editor of this series, for his support, encouragement, and patience; to my academic colleagues Duncan Forrester, Robin Gill, and Alan Lewis for their helpful suggestions and advice; and especially to many colleagues in the parochial and nonparochial ministries for the wealth of case material they so willingly supplied at my request. For reasons of confidentiality they must all remain anonymous. Without their help the arguments of this book could easily have remained floating free from the realities of modern pastoral care. There is perhaps a paradox in using the experience of this professional group to illustrate the limitations of professionalism, but I hope, nevertheless, that my fellow ministers will find in the ensuing pages much that is illuminative and supportive of their pastoral work. Finally, I am deeply indebted to Elma Webster for many hours of patient work on a much corrected manuscript.

Alastair V. Campbell
New College, Edinburgh.
January, 1984.

CHAPTER 1

_____

A Kind of Loving

When all is said and done the increase of . . . love of God and neighbor remains the purpose and the hope of our preaching of the gospel, of all our church organization and activity, of all our ministry.

H. Richard Niebuhr,
The Purpose of the Church and Its Ministry

Pastoral care is, in essence, surprisingly simple. It has one fundamental aim: to help people know love, both as something to be received and as something to give. The summary by Jesus of all the Law and the Prophets in two great Old Testament texts on love (Lev. 19:18; Deut. 6:5) tells us, as H. Richard Niebuhr suggests, all we need to know about the task of ministry. Yet the most simple things are often also the most elusive. We constantly lose sight of love, obscuring it with our anxieties and self-deceptions. We fail both to receive and to give love, because its simplicity seems so much more demanding than the complexities we have woven around our daily encounters with others. We are so conscious of ambiguity, exploitation, and egoism in relationships that we doubt the relevance of such a simple aim.

John is, it seems, beyond hope. In his early thirties, he is divorced, unemployed (and unemployable), with a chronic heart condition, a heavy addiction to alcohol, and a tendency to become violent when drunk. His father died when John was six, but his mother concealed the news from him until he found out by accident at age fourteen. He spent most of his teen-age years in institutions ranging from

11

children's homes to reform schools. He has virtually no education, has never had regular employment, and is almost permanently depressed, regularly taking drug overdoses. Whenever help is offered to him he rebels against it, seeking to undermine any chance of progress. Yet he constantly reappears in the church vestry or at the manse, expressing remorse and pleading for help.

Pastoral care is about helping people like John to give and receive love, to find their way out of the wilderness of their own and others' making, before it is too late for any help. Yet how is it to be done? Is ordinary friendship enough? John rebuffs or sabotages every friendship offered, by making impossible demands or by a deluge of broken promises and maudlin, uncontrollable contrition. Perhaps he should be given psychiatric help or be counseled and supported by a social worker. But he has long since run out of good will in those quarters! Classed as an inadequate personality, he is no longer welcome as a patient or client. Then, can the offer of pastoral care help, when simple friendship or skilled agency work has failed? This is the challenge in the seeming simplicity of the love command. How can we bring love to people who cannot even love themselves? And how can we change our society so that people like John are not rejected as beyond help? We seem to be very close to the "impossible ideal" described by Reinhold Niebuhr in his book, *An Interpretation of Christian Ethics:*

> This absolutism and perfectionism of Jesus' love ethic sets itself uncompromisingly not only against the natural self-regarding impulses, but against the necessary prudent defenses of the self, required because of the egoism of others.[1]

It may be tempting, when the radical demand of the Christian gospel is fully perceived, to try to spiritualize the love command, divorcing it from the psychological complexities of disturbed people and the glaring inadequacies of our social institutions. Divine love (agape) may be seen as a transcendent, superhuman power which is merely "channeled" through human helpers, but which depends on God's free grace alone to effect salvation.[2] Yet, this is hardly much help in the day-to-day exercise of pastoral care. We may readily admit that we need a power greater than our own to love truly and, especially, to persevere in love. But how does such transcendent love work through us? Surely it cannot be a purely arbitrary exercise of divine power. There must be ways in which we can open ourselves to that power and ways in which we can block it. This compels us to find a way of characterizing the human relationships in which pastoral care is offered.[3]

> Madge loved to talk to ministers and priests about her voices. Her own pastor had committed suicide in tragic circumstances, and her voices told her that this was a sign that the end of the world was near. When the hospital chaplain talked to Madge he did not challenge directly what her voices were saying, but gently persuaded her to talk about herself and about her own life before she had felt this call to proclaim the voices' message. Madge revealed a deep shame about, and hatred of, her own womanhood. She longed to be a man and felt dirty and guilty whenever her menstrual period came. She expected to be tortured by "communist queers" for the sin of being a woman and for sexual experience, which she regarded as unforgivable sin.

The person who would help Madge in her profound self-hatred must find a way of leading her to the knowledge of God's love for her *as she is*. No doubt, like John, Madge needs psychiatric treatment for her extreme disturbance, but (also like John) she needs some kind of steady companionship which can support her, despite all her strange ideas and her self-hatred. Madge needs something very simple, but also something that is not easy to find—a consistent and patient concern for her as a person of worth. The love that Madge needs will come from a healing relationship that counteracts whatever anxieties fuel her hatred of her femininity. That relationship must be embodied in a person who can be close in body to her without threatening her sexually. God's love of each of us equally needs to be expressed bodily. It is always incarnate love.

The dilemmas that John and Madge raise for anyone who would seek to offer them help bring me to my central concern in this book. Pastoral care seems to be a kind of friendship, an offer of a loving relationship. Yet "friendship" seems too weak a word to convey the difficulties we encounter in trying to mediate love to those who are deeply estranged from it. Some kind of consistency and skill is required in order to move from our natural aptitude for sympathy to the arduous task of genuine care and to the transformation of our society. Perhaps pastoral care has to be a kind of professional activity, like psychotherapy or casework or depth counseling. Yet, there may be a danger that if we professionalize pastoral care, we will lose the spontaneity and the simplicity that characterize love. Can we translate the command of Jesus to love thy neighbor simply into the instruction to become a trained counselor? This seems a poor translation indeed. Yet the naiveté of those who try to put love into practice without the discipline of training is also obvious. The issues involved cannot be quickly answered, either by abjuring professionalism or by wholeheartedly embracing it. Instead, we must look more closely at the nature of the Christian vocation to love and at the strengths and weaknesses of the professional approach. In the remainder of this chapter I shall begin this task by exploring the various meanings ascribed to the terms "love" and "professionalism."

THE MEANINGS OF LOVE

Madge's inward fears reveal the most common associations an appeal to love evokes: love as sexual response. When we speak of "lovers" we nearly always imply a sexual union, and books advertised as "love manuals" are unlikely to be thought of as handbooks on Christian ethics! Love and sex have become synonymous in a culture obsessed with physical appearance and sensual gratification. Yet we must beware of the opposite extreme, which puts Christian love in a wholly different realm from such physical love.

The biblical context of the command to love God with heart and soul and mind, and one's neighbor as oneself, is the parable of the Good Samaritan. Like all Jesus' parables this gives a fully human and earthy character to his teaching. The parable describes robbery and physical assault, pride and religious prejudice, and a courageous and wholly practical form of loving. It locates love of neighbor in the midst of all the risks of life, both physical and emotional. Moreover, when Jesus encounters condemnation of sexual misdemeanors (Luke 7:36–50; John 8:1–11), his quiet responses reveal the narrow perception of those who quickly judge. He does not shrink from the bodily manifestations of love, yet he also sees beyond them. His teaching starts with the physical, but it is not trapped by it. He communicates by gesture, word, and action the complexity of love.

We need to see, then, that there are many meanings to love, and each is important in its own way. Here Abraham Maslow's "hierarchy of human needs" can provide a useful structure for describing the complexity of love.[4] Our earliest experiences of love are related to simple survival. Our parent's love nourishes and protects us and gives that sense of security so essential to our emotional well-being. The experience of family life and friendship provides the love that tells us that we have a place in the world and are valued for what we have to give to others. From this sense of belonging and esteem we reach out to values that transcend our own needs, finding the wider world of others' demands and gifts, which enlightens and challenges our self-centered vision. This is the progression that the command to love God and neighbor promotes. It begins from our bodily vulnerability and tension; it reminds us of the joys of bodily fulfillment, parenthood, and personal friendships; and it reveals a kingdom whose borders are wider than those of personal satisfaction, family, and the company of those we like.

Thus the love we call agape takes us beyond the comfort and security of the place we have made for ourselves on earth, leading to a rougher, more risky way. It does not deny the goodness of the former, but it will not leave us wholly contented with it. Outside the warm circle of personal friendship there is the needy neighbor who is also Christ (Matt. 25:31–46). Agape, Christian love, perpetually unsettles us in the name of a greater peace.

Such a view of love is opposed to the spiritualizing of Christianity which implies that Christian love has no concern for social injustices or for the physical and mental distress of individuals. Love is one, in this view. At the same time, the equation of love's aims with physical well-being, psychological maturity, or political liberation is also opposed. However important and necessary they may be, these aims can be only part of the whole picture of God's kingdom. The transcendence of love questions every identification of human aspiration with the final kingdom.[5]

> Di was at the forefront of the peace movement in her church. If there was a march, Di was there, colorful as ever with her striking looks and bright clothes, singing the songs of freedom and cheerfully submitting to police harassment and the occasional arrest for civil disobedience. Yet she often wondered what she was really doing. Her husband regarded her behavior as "weird" and was threatening to leave her unless she gave up her political activity. Her children, who were approaching teen-age years, seemed very mixed up and in a constant state of strife with one another. And she, herself? Was she sure that her Christian belief required this political activity? Perhaps (she secretly thought) these marches are just a way of escape for me.

Di's self-questioning is of the greatest importance in the struggle to find the meaning of Christian love. She senses that love is one, that a force that drives her away from family conflicts in an identification with political causes may not be all that it appears. Such perception is to her credit. Those who scornfully watch her marching, secure in their own respectable behavior, could be further from love. Living comfortably in an unjust world, they do not hear the unsettling call of love at all. They want peace without a sword, failing to see that true peace never comes from compromise or from the concealment of conflict.

We begin to see the rich texture of the command to love. But what gives it unity? Paul Tillich has suggested that every form of love seeks "reunion of the separated."[6] At a basic level our actions are driven by desire (*epithymia*), which leads to physical closeness and sexual union. The next level of love (eros) is the pursuit of that which attracts us, expressed in its purest form as the quest for beauty. Then comes friendship (*philia*), the meeting of personalities in shared experience. From these forms of love there comes a dynamism which can then be used by neighbor love (agape). Neighbor love seeks to overcome divisiveness and strife between all individual selves, to reunite the separated through justice.

Parallel to the unity of the love of neighbor is the unity of the love of God. To the weak, God offers nourishment and protection; but to those who see themselves as mighty, he demands humility (Luke 1:51–53). To know God's love is to find great comfort, but it is also to be driven out of our self-centered pride and self-sufficiency. The love that sustains is also the love that chides and provokes. The language of God's call to love is full of action and movement—go, seek, follow, baptize, heal, preach.

This tension between comfort and challenge in the love of God suffuses pastoral care with a volatile spirit, which resists the confinement of the conventional and expected. In an age trapped in moralism it may well mediate accepting love, but in a self-satisfied age it will reinstate love's judgment of the proud. It can make alliance with professions that give skilled care to people's diseased bodies and disturbed minds, but it has lost all identity if it never questions the assumptions of these professions. Pastoral care constantly seeks illumination by surprising and refreshing visions of God's love.

Mrs. A. was an elderly woman who had been a staunch Baptist all her days. She had a quiet fortitude that sustained her through many difficult times, including the loss of her husband to whom she had been married for forty-two years. For some time she had suffered from a serious heart condition which required an operation if her life was to be saved. At the urging of her doctors and her son Mrs. A. had the operation, but she felt she was doing it only to please them. She did not fear death and she longed to be reunited with her husband. Mrs. A. never regained full consciousness after the operation and she required life-support systems to stay alive. Her condition neither deteriorated nor improved, and it was decided that the life support should not be continued if she began to show signs of brain death. The chaplain who had been visiting her before the operation felt that Mrs. A. was holding on to life out of a sense of duty to others. Sensing that she could still hear what was being said to her, the chaplain whispered, "Mrs. A., it's all right for you to die, you know. God does not mind you letting go." Shortly afterwards neurological tests showed a flat EEG and the life-support system was removed.

For the chaplain to go against the medical life-sustaining endeavor was a bold, indeed possibly a lethal, step. Yet love seemed to demand it. To care for Mrs. A. was to set her free to die, letting her faith in a loving God have its natural outcome in a peaceful end. The chaplain's pastoral care had its own answerability, its own reference points, which set it cross-grained to the smooth operation of the medical regimen of care. Of course, a humane medicine also knows when to let people die, but frequently the prophetic voice of independent pastoral care is needed to save medicine from an enslavement to its own technology.

So Christian love, as I have now reviewed it, gives a distinctive character to pastoral care. Medicine, social work, and nursing are practiced within the broad context of the physical and behavioral sciences. They take for granted certain values such as health, freedom from pain and disability, and the pursuit of happiness for the individual, and they seek scientifically based methods of implementing these values. Since love is one, the ministry of pastoral care can celebrate and support the many achievements of such caring acts, but it is not limited to the goals they define or to the ultimate values they espouse. The context within which it works is not that of science, but of sacrament, prayer, and prophecy, all of which can turn the values of humanistic love into only proximate goals. Life is good, but prayer seeks a transfiguration of the ordinary into the eternal; the prophet calls the city to justice but also foresees a heavenly city yet to appear; the priest knows that it is good to rebuild the walls of Jerusalem, but also serves him who was crucified *outside* the city walls; in Baptism and in the Eucharist the symbols of life and rejoicing mingle with those of death and repentance. These shades of light and dark, of certainty and uncertainty, cover a mystery that defies rational description. Love's simplicity cannot be captured in the categories of science, and pastoral care lacks the security of a secure place in the earthly city.

THE NATURE OF
PROFESSIONALISM

This picture of pastoral care in the service of love may seem to rule out the idea that professionalism has a place within it. To some extent, however, this is because the true nature of professionalism is not immediately obvious. The term "profession" has undergone a transformation in modern times. Originally it referred to the public declaration of faith associated with a life of religious obedience. Thus a "clerk in holy orders" (cleric or clergyman[7]) can be seen as the original professional person. Prior to the Renaissance and Reformation clerics held a monopoly not only of priestly functions but also of most medical and all legal functions. The idea of a secular profession is still alien in many non-Western cultures, where a priestly caste may also carry out healing and quasi-legal functions. In industrialized societies, however, specialist occupations or "professions" have emerged and risen to such prominence that they now provide the norm for the concept of the professional person, as opposed to the tradesperson, artisan, or unskilled worker. Thus what was originally a distinction in terms of religous and secular occupations has become changed into a social class distinction, to be understood largely (but not exclusively) in socioeconomic terms. Moreover, modern societies are witnessing a process of increasing *professionalization*, in which more and more occupational groups are claiming the status of profession and are seeking the same prestige and privileges as those enjoyed by the established professions, such as medicine or law.

To speak of professionalism and pastoral care in any intelligible way, we need to understand something of the historical and sociological background to the high esteem in which "a professional approach" is held in our present age. It would be easy to dismiss professionalism as irrelevant to a genuinely committed pastoral care, or—equally unthinkingly—to support it wholeheartedly as the only responsible approach to a ministry of care for others. Instead we must recognize the *moral ambiguity* of the claim to professional status. Only then can we make a balanced assessment of its relevance to pastoral care. In the remainder of this chapter I shall attempt to convey an impression of this modern phenomenon of professionalism by summarizing three approaches to the sociology of professions: the trait approach; the functionalist approach; the power-struggle approach. This will prepare the ground for my discussion in the next chapter of the relationship between vocation and profession in pastoral care.

The Trait Approach

This first approach attempts to identify common traits among occupational groups that would be widely acknowledged as professions. A typical list of such traits would be (1) a body of knowledge and associated skills that require a lengthy period of education and training; (2) tests of knowledge and competence before qualification to practice; (3) colleague supervision and discipline; (4) adherence to an ethical code that stresses service to others above personal gain.[8] These traits are drawn in the first instance from the so-called "learned" professions of divinity, law, and medicine, but they would also fit most of the groups who have more recently set up qualifying associations, such as accountants, architects, nurses, social workers, and school teachers. There are, however, obvious problems in such an approach. First, the criteria are so wide that virtually any group that has specialist knowledge and skills can claim to be included.[9] If, however, the criteria are to be narrowed, it is not clear how this is to be done. The trait approach offers no grounds for its choice other than those of use and custom. Why should the "learned" professions be the normative ones, just because they are the oldest?

The Functionalist Approach

One way of establishing more rigorous criteria is to inquire into the social functions that the emergence of professionalism appears to fulfill.[10] This functionalist approach describes the loss of close family or tribal loyalties in large urban societies resulting in the need for specialist helpers who can be relied upon, even though they are strangers to the person seeking help. Two features of professionalism are regarded as meeting this social need: trustworthiness and emotional neutrality. Trustworthiness depends upon both competence and adherence to a code of conduct. Emotional neutrality is ensured by selection, training, and (if need be) discipline of delinquent practitioners who cross the boundary of the professional relationship. The greater the vulnerability of the individual seeking help, the more important it is that these features are institutionalize d in professional groups.

This account provides a powerful rationale for describing those occupational groups who provide legal help and health care as "professions." The clients of lawyers do not have sufficient knowledge of the law to know how they should deal with a difficult legal situation and they need advice from someone who can give an informed and detached view. Even more so, the physically or mentally ill need trustworthy and competent helpers who will deal with them according to need, not according to profitability, and will not themselves lose objectivity by becoming too emotionally involved. Other groups claiming "professional" status may not be justified in doing so because their clients are able to inform themselves sufficiently to be discriminating buyers of services, and are able to protect themselves emotionally against exploitation. Thus, for example, plumbers would not be "professional" in this specific sense, because their clients can protect themselves against exploitation and malpractice, but doctors, school teachers, and social workers would be "professional" because they deal with people in a vulnerable state.

The Power-Struggle Approach

Advocates of the third approach to professionalism criticize the other approaches for being both idealistic and ahistorical. The trait approach, it is argued, fails to account for the phenomenon of professional*ization,* which constantly alters the lists of traits of self-described professions. The functionalist approach merely describes an ideal state of affairs in which occupational groups are perfectly adapted to the needs of the vulnerable, but it fails to explain sufficiently why professions attain such power and social status and why they seek to retain it, even when clients become increasingly capable of caring for themselves. The power-struggle approach argues that the reputation for trustworthiness and consistency of the established professions brings them major social advantages. An occupational group such as the medical profession, which has gained state registration, is granted a monopoly within the profitable market of health care provision together with a high degree of autonomy in selection, training, control of malpractice, and limitation of entry to the profession. This represents considerable power, both in terms of earning capacity and in the determination of the conditions of work and the future patterns of professional practice. Thus, to be recognized as a profession is to gain major social and economic advantages compared with other groups who hold only an employee status within institutions controlled by others. The power-struggle analysis concludes that the ethical codes of professions, far from being disinterested expressions of altruism, are "campaign documents in the struggle for privilege and power".[11] The trust the service orientation engenders results in gaining or maintaining a much-prized political advantage, professional autonomy.

Conclusions

Each of these approaches has a certain persuasive force. It is not my intention to arbitrate between them. I simply conclude that the modern concept of profession encompasses many semantic and moral ambiguities. It is not at all clear what is being described when we say that an activity is "professional." At the simplest level, perhaps we are offering a contrast with "amateur," by which we mean work by the unpaid and untrained. But some activities—for example, sports or fine arts—benefit greatly from the dedication and innovation of amateurs. (It could well be that the style of pastoral care I have been describing earlier would benefit from the freshness of the amateur approach.) On the other hand, the alleged drawback of amateur work is that it cannot be consistently relied upon. Here the notion of professional control and responsibility can be seen as the important factor. The professional is not merely an individual working in isolation. Professional work reflects an ethos acquired through years of training and experience, which provides the individual practitioner with both support and control. Yet it is precisely here that the moral ambiguity of professionalism is most evident. As we have seen, professionalism possibly benefits the professional at least as much as the client. Professional codes of ethics may not be as altruistic as they at first appear. They tend to underwrite the inviolable moral status of the profession and to avoid any kind of radical social critique that might question established practice. As long as professionalism brings socioeconomic advantages to practitioners they are unlikely to seek societal change or to encourage criticism of its effectiveness. Professionalism becomes a self-perpetuating monopoly.

We are left, then, with a dilemma in respect to pastoral care. In the past, pastoral care was obviously a professional activity, at least in some sense, since it was carried out by the original profession, the clergy. We cannot assume, however, that this applies to the present. We have seen recently the growth of "a profession within a profession," the trained and accredited pastoral counselor. At the same time, the question of the ministry of the whole church, not just of specialist groups within it, is being constantly raised. Will it be from increased professionalization or from the use of the variety of gifts within the membership as a whole that an innovative and responsive pastoral care will come? Undoubtedly professionalism has both great advantages and great dangers. We shall have to consider how profession and vocation are to be related to one another within the context of the call that comes to all Christians. Is the ministry of love of God and neighbor aided or hindered by the ordering of the church's task through the setting apart of professional ministers? What is the function of this group in relation to the whole "people of God" from which they are drawn? Can love flourish when order, organization, accreditation, and authorized roles become dominant in pastoral care? Conversely, can it survive at all if there are no structures through which it can be consistently expressed?

These are far from being questions of merely theoretical interest. Who will see Madge as a neighbor when her madness persists? Who will both tolerate and challenge John's childish and demanding behavior? Who will be willing to march alongside Di, but also be able to share in her inner turmoil? Who will be unafraid to sit with Mrs. A. as, following the light of her faith, she steps into the valley of shadows?

We must not be too hasty in describing such expressions of neighbor love as professional tasks, but they certainly require a discipline, a consistency, and a wisdom that does not come easily to any of us. We shall have to consider how the strengths of professionalism can be made available to all who profess to follow Christ, the man who opened himself to others at the cost of suffering, death, and descent into the very depths of hell. Such a vocation can scarcely be fulfilled merely by good intentions or by the ebb and flow of feelings of sympathy and benevolence. From some source, then, we must find perseverance that justifies trust in our love.

CHAPTER 2

Profession
and
Vocation

*As soon as I think of my neighbor, all vocations no longer stand on a
common plane, but a certain vocation comes to the fore as mine.*
Gustaf Wingren, *Luther on Vocation*

We were left at the conclusion of the last chapter with many
unanswered questions. We saw, on the one hand, the call to
Christian love, which demands a rich, self-giving, and risky response to the neighbor; we saw, on the other, the ambiguous
phenomenon of professionalism, with its apparent benefits for
people in need, but no less apparent benefits for the professional
practitioner. Which is the true world of pastoral care? In this
chapter I shall move closer to an answer to this question by
surveying the concept of vocation, as it is understood within the
context of Christian faith, and then by considering to what extent
professionalism may be an appropriate response to that vocation.

VOCATION, GIFTS, AND
GRATITUDE

"Vocation" derives its meaning from belief in a *vocatio*, a call
from a Creator God who molds humanity and all nature with
loving intent, seeking the flourishing and fulfillment of all created
things. This active and provident God is described by Martin
Luther in a characteristically direct way: "God himself will milk
the cows through him whose vocation that is."[1] In other words, to
find one's vocation is to find how one's abilities fit into the benevo-
lent work of an ever-present God. The contented cow, skillfully

milked, produces through the milkman's or milkmaid's labor nourishment for the neighbor. God's call for flourishing is fulfilled in this simple fashion.

Such an idyllic picture, however, is often seen as a fleeting vision in the realities of a fallen world. The destructive forces of sin fragment the harmonies and natural rhythms of God's good work and the vision of God in creation is lost. The neighbor then becomes a competitor, a rival, or a victim; the natural world is exploited for material wealth, fought over, and progressively denuded of resources; God is seen by humankind "east of Eden," not as loving presence, but as a baleful and uncaring despot or as a mere irrelevance. In the strident and shadowed world of sin there is no sense of receiving spontaneously offered gifts and no impulse of gratitude that can lift one's eyes to the neighbor's need.

> Jane is anorexic—a "classic case." All seemed to go well for her—she graduated from college with honors, and before that she was president of her high school class, good at athletics, and strikingly good-looking.
>
> Jane went to college because it was the "thing to do." After college she did research but lost interest, and then took a secretarial course, graduating at the top of her class.
>
> She lives in isolation and finds it hard to relate to people. There are no close friends and few she trusts. Somehow she is unable to enter into any meaningful friendship, but professes to be searching for faith. She has been in and out of several hospitals and taken "cures" from several people. Her hopes are raised continually and then shattered.
>
> She has classic symptoms, but is unable to see any meaning in life or existence.
>
> She says that she wants to be normal, but through the last ten years of her life she has gone from one crisis to another supported by her parents—whom she loathes.

Jane's deep unhappiness and sense of hopeless isolation are symbolic of the pervasive influence of failure, hopelessness, and tragedy in human life. Certainly her reaction is an extreme one. In her despair and self-hatred she is starving to death the graceful and athletic body which was her unsought inheritance, and she can find no creative outlet for her natural intelligence. Others may see her as fortunate—clever, pretty, successful—but, in her crippling alienation from her parents and from her own body, Jane feels only loneliness and loathing. Her distressing (and probably lethal) condition is the final form of a disease that can affect us all. We sometimes feel gifted or free to love, but all too often we feel despised, resentful, and defensive. We can find our vocation only when our eyes are opened to see our gifts and their relationship to our neighbor's needs.

It is because sin is so pervasive and so destructive that an understanding of vocation requires a move from a theology of creation to a theology of grace and redemption. In the state of alienation symbolized by Jane's distress we are constantly seeking someone to blame for our unhappiness (ourselves, our parents, or God perhaps). We imagine that finding a culprit will bring us some peace. But grace does not apportion blame; it simply sets aside the language of victims and culprits, of excuses and lack of excuse, of guilt and punishment; it takes us to a radiant place of hope for the future and delight in the opportunities of love. Gustaf Wingren, in his summary of Luther's writing on vocation, expresses this sense of grace in a few powerful sentences:

> There is nothing more delightful and lovable on earth than one's neighbor. Love does not think about doing works, it finds joy in people. . . . Love never does something because it has to. It is permitted to act. And earth "with its trees and grass" is the site of man's vocation.[2]

So grace restores us to the created world and to our neighbor. The Christian vocation is a response to grace that takes us back to "our place"[3] in the world and to a joy in caring for others. It is the response of people who were once captive, but now released (redeemed); who were estranged, but now find closeness (reconciled); whose world was shattered, but is now made whole (saved). This response rediscovers the goodness in creation and so restores a sense of vocation based on gifts and gratitude.

VOCATION AND MINISTRY

Within the context of a return to the world of living hope, where God's creative goodness is found, the narrower sense of Christian vocation can now be demarcated. This narrower sense is signified by the term "ministry." In Christian theology all such ministry takes its identity from Jesus Christ, the first and only true faithful minister. The vocation to ministry takes numerous forms but it revolves around one central theme—servanthood. The term "ministry" is itself a translation of the Greek *diakonia,* meaning the task of serving at table. In John's Gospel we are offered a powerful image. While others squabble about status and rank, the leader casts aside his outer garments and performs the menial task of foot washing (John 13:1–17). In the Synoptic Gospels the suffering servant of Isaiah's prophecy is used with great power as a key to understanding Jesus' seemingly passive and useless death. In the letter to the Philippians the humility, the self-emptying, of God's Son is seen as the one royal route to restoring glory in creation (Phil. 2:5–11). And in the letter to the Hebrews, which has its roots deep in the Jewish temple ritual, there is found a new kind of priestly service where priest, sacrifice, and the yearned-for holiness become one in the patient humanity of Jesus (Heb. 6:14–15). All these images of Christ's servanthood or ministry are summed up in the basic symbol of Christianity, the cross, that ambivalent reminder of suffering and glory. To be a minister in the name of Jesus, as Jesus reminded his followers who sought an easier way, is to feel the weight of the cross on one's own shoulders.

Throughout Christian history the problems posed by this central theme of humble servanthood in Jesus' life and teaching have proved almost insuperable for the church that claims to follow him. Humility does not institutionalize well. It is a way of being and responding, not a social role or a set of defined tasks. Yet from the earliest times the church has required structures and people in authority in order to maintain and develop its community through a turbulent and often hazardous history. The problem is that the structures and the leaders then tend to become invested with importance and spiritual status well beyond their true function in the community of believers. Instead of being viewed as merely functionally necessary to ensure some kind of order and continuity,[4] the nominated or ordained leaders become paradigmatic for all Christian ministry, and those Christians who are not ordained become viewed as "lesser" Christians, followers of human leaders rather than followers of Christ. Clerical status thus seems to place a barrier between Christ, the suffering servant who summons *all* to follow him, and those people whose way of following is not to seek office in the church. Yet it could well be that the person who modestly, humbly, and quietly tries to follow Christ in a "secular calling" is closer to the reality of the suffering and danger that Christ warned must come to those who walk in his way.

In *Why Priests?* Hans Küng has summed up well the essence of Christian ministry:

> The specific factor is not that one enjoys an "office" in the church . . . what matters is that one is a "believer" pure and simple: that is a person who believes, listens, serves, loves and hopes.[5]

The string of verbs that Küng uses to describe the basic ministry of all Christians—"believes, listens, serves, loves, hopes"— provides a vivid summary of the ministry of pastoral care in which all share. Because of the grace that redeems, reconciles, and saves, the "ordinary Christian" is given the patience to listen and to serve and the confidence to love and to hope. Without these qualities there will be no genuine helping of others. To have in addition a recognized office (of priest or deacon, presbyter or bishop) is no advantage for the fundamental task of humble love, and may indeed constitute an obstacle to be overcome. As Paul puts it in the First Letter to the Corinthians, the most eloquent public speaker is making empty noise if love is lacking (1 Cor. 13:1–2).

It may seem, then, that to speak correctly of vocation and ministry in pastoral care is to reject totally the professional model. The whole force of my argument up to this point has been to contrast office and expertise with humility and simplicity. Yet something will be lost if we rest content with what has been said so far. It is *possible* to be an ordained minister without being seduced by the notion of superior status. Similarly it is *possible* to attempt to meet a professional ideal of leadership in a way that emphasizes not power, but service. There is a way of being a professional that is vocational in character, just as (to use Luther's example) there is a way of milking a cow.

THE ORDAINED MINISTRY AND PROFESSIONALISM

The following case suggests where the strengths of a pastoral care vested in a professional ministry might lie:

> Sandra is not a member of the congregation, nor are her parents. She simply called to ask if the minister would baptize her baby. She was not married. We smiled, talked about the baby and the support given her by the rest of the family, and the baptism was arranged. No conditions attached, no "ifs" or "buts."
>
> Sandra found a small house in another part of the city. The local minister was asked to call—and did, and kept in touch. It took Sandra a whole year to become confident enough to leave her child in the nursery, and to go to worship herself. It was another year after that when the original pastor received this letter:
>
>> I am about to write probably the biggest "thank you" letter of my life. I don't know if you'll remember me, but my name is Sandra. I had a baby called John whom you christened. . . . When I moved here you wrote to Mr. Smith, but it took me a whole year to go to church, and then it was only to please him. But after a few weeks I found that I wanted to go . . . and now everything seems to have fallen into place and I realize that God loves me. . . . That is why I am writing to you, because it was you who took the first step in helping me to find God. I will always be grateful for it.

We can see from this example that the help the two ordained ministers gave Sandra was of a kind specifically related to their social role and to their office within the church. Their willingness to accept her and her baby (especially as this was powerfully symbolized in the sacrament of Baptism) communicated an image of the Christian congregation and of God's love to her in a manner that no other church member could have done so effectively. The representative role of the ordained minister became the vehicle for an expression of loving, accepting concern.

This aspect of professionalism may be seen to be related to its root meaning of a public declaration, a statement of intent, a vow (*professio*). The ordained minister is, more obviously than other Christians, an "ambassador for Christ" (2 Cor. 5:20), a person who regularly communicates in word and action the nature of the commitment that all Christians share. For good or ill, the way in which the ordained minister deals with people is taken to be representative of Christians as a group. Thus, as Anthony Russell has pointed out in his study of clergy in the Church of England,[6] the minister shares with other professions a blurring of the distinction between work and nonwork. Person and occupational role are not clearly separated. Rather, the sort of person the ordained minister (or doctor, or nurse, or school teacher) appears to be to those who are seeking help always affects the quality of help that is received. As members of what Paul Halmos has called the "personal service professions,"[7] ministers carry both the burden and the opportunity of being symbolizers of value. They are expected to embody the ideals for which their profession stands, whether concern for health and care of the sick, or for knowledge and the spread of education, or for love and forgiveness and the rescuing of the needy and lost. They are required to be not only efficient and knowledgeable, but trustworthy and genuinely committed to the professed task. In the sense, "personal service professionals" are never off duty.

Yet it is precisely here that we also see the dangers of professionalism. The demand to be a living symbol elevates the individual to an unrealistic, and often intolerable, "heroic" level. The weakness and evident humanity of the practitioner cannot be admitted for fear of betraying the ideal. The result is often a great cost to the personal integrity, family life, and emotional health of the representative person who attempts to meet every expectation and a demoting of the pastoral role of "ordinary people." The clergy often feel denied the possibility of anger, sexual de-

sire, and times of disbelief. Though offering relief and reassur-
ance to sinners, they cannot permit themselves to be one of that
number without excessive guilt.[8] The symbolic role has virtually
engulfed the person.

PROFESSION, FUNCTION,
AND ROLE

It is at this point that the symbolic, nonrational elements of
professionalism need to be counterbalanced by the more rational,
functional elements. In *The Clerical Profession* Russell has documented in a richly detailed and often amusing way the different
phases through which the social status of the clergy of the Church
of England has passed from the eighteenth century to the present
day. The agricultural prosperity of the eighteenth century turned
the impoverished parish clergy into relatively prosperous members of the landed gentry, making a clerical living an attractive
proposition for "dull and decent"[9] sons of the squirearchy. Fresh
social changes in the nineteenth century, however, led to an
emphasis on professionalism, where not only income and social
class, but competence and knowledge became important if the
clergy were to maintain their position. Russell's description of the
nineteenth-century "professional man" (women were not, of
course, permitted to enter the professions until very late in that
century) provides an illuminating background to a modern understanding of the clerical role:

> It was the professional man, gentlemanly but highly skilled, cultured
> but technically capable, conscious of the service ethic yet making a
> good livelihood . . . who was the quintessential self-made man, and
> who became the cultural hero of late-nineteenth-century English
> society.[10]

Russell's observations apply more widely than his specific study of
England and the Anglican Church. While it is true that in other
countries and other churches the social class factor has been less
prominent, it seems likely that the "skilled gentleman" ideal has
had a pervasive effect. In the twentieth century the emphasis on
gentility in professionalism has begun to decline, but as a result

there has been an ever-growing emphasis on knowledge, skill, and training. The professional person in our era earns respect and social position through competence and esoteric knowledge, acquired through a lengthy process of specialized education. Once that position is achieved, the professional becomes a member of a favored class. In the phrase of one sociologist, we have witnessed in modern times the "rise of the meritocracy."[11]

Here, then, we see the emergence of an apparently rational foundation for professionalism, the professional as the trained and accredited expert. The effect of this social trend on the education of the clergy has been obvious. Whereas in the past theological education often consisted of a broadly liberal education in the arts followed by exposure to the classical disciplines of theology, history, and biblical studies, now there is an ever-increasing emphasis on acquiring professional skills in preaching, administration, education, leading of worship, and counseling. The minister as a "man of learning" who picked up skills on the job is being replaced by the model of the modern professional—carefully selected, methodically trained, and tested for competence before accreditation by the professional group. The men and women who now enter the ordained ministry can see themselves as the near equals of their contemporaries in medicine, social work, or law so far as professional formation is concerned.[12]

Is it possible that the development of expertise in the modern clergy can help avoid the pitfalls of the "representative Christian" symbolic role? We observed in the previous chapter that, in the functionalist analysis of professionalism, the professional offers not only trustworthiness but also "affective neutrality." Perhaps then the "new professionals" in the clergy, alerted by their exposure to clinical pastoral education, will be able to offer an appropriate emotional relationship to people who seek their help—one that saves the client from inappropriate dependence and the professional from "burnout."[13]

Molly is in her middle fifties. Since early childhood the frailty and failure of all her relationships to mother and maiden aunts who brought her up left her with a deep mistrust of life and terror of death. When anyone close to her dies she experiences a traumatic sense of separation. She views her own death with horror, which has at least had the benefit of preventing her from committing suicide. She has adopted two main lines of action to help her cope with this:

First, she has always surrounded herself with a string of professionals—psychiatrist, community physician, nature cure doctor, psychologist, minister—most of whom find it impossible to meet her demands on their time and skill. She is thoroughly hypochondriac and can see symptoms that are not evident to others and that make her panic because she is "dying."

Second, she tests such relationships as she does have to the breaking point in order to "prove" her thesis that all relationships eventually fail you and let you down.

In responding to Molly, the completely untrained person will be tested to destruction, and the friendship will in the end be made to fail. Usually, professionally trained counselors spot the nature of the problem and suspect that here is a person who cannot receive help. Some have extricated themselves at this point so as not to waste their time. Some have not!

People like Molly reveal why professionalism, at least in the sense of "affective neutrality," can be convincingly defended as a necessary attribute of pastoral ministry. Without it, the well-meaning provider of pastoral care is likely, it seems, to be "tested to destruction." The same may apply, though in a less obvious way, to the other functions that have devolved onto the ordained clergy—preaching, conduct of worship, administration, and organization of the congregation.[14] All these functions seem to benefit from the skills and emotional control derived from training and experience, which characterizes professional work in other contexts.

In his book, *Profession: Minister,* J. D. Glasse has argued strongly that the attributes of professionalism belong to the ministry, not only because traditionally the ministry has been regarded as a profession, but also because professionalism is functionally appropriate to the task. Glasse lists five characteristics that the ministry shares with other professions: education, skill, association with an institution, responsibility, and dedication. Glasse goes on to describe how these characteristics affect the exercise of the various functions of ministry. In the case of pastoral care this entails the use of both theological and psychological knowledge to develop specifically pastoral skills which are used in service of the church. These skills are exercised responsibly through seeking adequate training and supervision, but paradoxically, it is the dedication of the minister to love of God and neighbor that can ensure that limits are placed on overinvolvement and that cooperation of others is sought in the pastoral task. The minister as professional, says Glasse, takes a "calculated risk" in this regard:

> In becoming educated, expert, institutional, and responsible the clergyman runs the risk of losing his dedication. But it is a risk that some must run if we are to have clergy equal to the tasks of the Church in the twentieth century. Warm hearts are needed, but they are not enough. Cool heads and steady hands—marks of professional competence—are also required.[15]

We see in Glasse's exposition a combination of what were characterized in chapter 1 as the *trait* and the *functionalist* approaches to professionalism. His argument is perhaps at its weakest when he makes bold claims for the social usefulness of the alleged professionalism of modern ministers. Two recent sociological studies of the clergy in the Church of England, Anthony Russell's *The Clerical Profession* and R. Towler and A. P. M. Coxon's *The Fate of the Anglican Clergy*,[16] have suggested that the clergy as an occupational group are becoming increasingly "marginalized," in the sense that many of their historic functions have been taken over by other groups, and the decline in church membership has limited their influence to a shrinking minority of the population. Russell notes that there is a greater emphasis on pastoral care in contemporary ministry than at any other time, but he doubts whether the continuation of a full-time professional ministry can provide the necessary resources for exercising it. He sees part of the problem of the loss of effectiveness of the church in modern society to be that its ministry "has become trapped in an increasingly problematic institutional form."[17] In similar vein, Towler and Coxon regard the ministry as "professional only in a sense long, long extinct,"[18] and recommend that instead of claiming an unsupportable professional status the clergy should use their position of marginality to provide a prophetic witness to society. Thus, because he fails to allow for social change, Glasse's emphasis on the functional advantages of professionalism in ministry may be seen as mistaken. The more effective ministry could be one that eschews the attribution of professionalism. Society is moving on, and the historical role of the clergy as professionals is no longer a secure one in either Britain or the United States.

PASTORAL CARE AND LEADERSHIP

If, then, we are in a genuinely new situation in our era, how might the churches organize themselves effectively to promote the ministry of pastoral care? Does it still make sense to centralize all the ministerial (servant) functions of the church in one designated individual, however well trained, however carefully prepared? This question should not be regarded as merely one about practicalities. It requires more adventurous theological thinking about the life of the modern church than may be implied by the bald assertion that the ordained clergy have had, and should continue to have, a representative function in all the church's work. Is this really how *diakonia* should be exercised in contemporary life?

The first issue to be resolved is the relationship between the whole people of God and the ordained clergy. Thomas C. Oden, in a recent major textbook on ministry entitled *Pastoral Theology: Essentials of Ministry,* has sought a renewed emphasis on the setting apart of the clergy by ordination. While opposing any kind of "triumphalist" account of the leadership exercised by the clergy, Oden nevertheless makes the ordained minister the principal actor in all the work of the church. Here is how Oden summarizes his viewpoint in relation to pastoral care:

> Although caring ministries are indeed a responsibility for the whole laity, the minister's care of souls (*cura animarum*) comes in the name

of the whole church, offering word, sacrament, counsel, corrective guidance, and empathy, not on the basis of his or her own personal insight, but on the basis of being called, prepared, ordained and authorized to representative ministry.[19]

This manner of approach to pastoral care entails the use of what Oden calls the "pivotal analogy" of shepherding as a way of describing the central position of leadership-in-service of the minister within the Christian congregation. Oden sees this shepherding position as "divinely commissioned"[20] and he regards his defense of it to be substantiated by the four classical sources for theological truth: Scripture, tradition, reason, and experience.[21]

There is no question that this approach to ministry in general and to pastoral care in particular has many centuries of Christian tradition on its side (as Oden's liberal use of the Christian classics amply demonstrates), but any appeal to Scripture, reason, or experience carries less weight. Modern biblical and theological scholarship has disclosed the rich diversity in the New Testament references to ministry and the cultural and historical influences that have brought about the forms of church leadership that we have inherited. As Küng has observed, the emphasis on "office" in the tradition is largely a legacy of the Constantine era, when roles in the Imperial Church had to be equated with positions in the Imperial Civil Service.[22] So far as the "pivotal analogy" of shepherding derived from the New Testament is concerned, references to Christian leaders as shepherds are rare and late (Eph. 4:11; 1 Pet. 5:2). It is Christ, in almost every instance, who is the bearer of that title (Mark 14:26–27 and par.; John 10; Heb. 13:20; 1 Pet. 2:25; Rev. 7:17), not his followers. Moreover, there is no single view of ministry in the New Testament documents. The diversity is well described by the New Testament scholar J. D. G. Dunn. Dunn observes that in the pre-Easter discipleship phase the concept of ministry is centered exclusively on Jesus. After the resurrection and Pentecost the first-generation Christians exhibit two diverging patterns:

> On the one hand, the early and somewhat chaotic charismatic free-
> dom of the Jerusalem church settled down into a more conservative
> pattern of church order borrowed from the synagogue; on the
> other, Paul vigorously advocated a much freer vision of charismatic
> community, where unity and maturity grew out of the living inter-
> play of gifts and ministries without dependence on any office or
> hierarchy.[23]

Dunn goes on to argue that the later stages of primitive Chris-
tainity, as evidenced in the New Testament documents, showed
even more diversity, with the pastoral epistles developing a blend
of Pauline and traditionally Jewish leadership forms, while John,
Hebrews, and Revelation all oppose representative office and
stress the *corporate* nature of priesthood and prophecy. The
Johannine literature in particular, according to Dunn, seems "to
preserve what we would call now a kind of conventicle or camp-
meeting or convention Christianity."[24]

In view of this New Testament diversity of approach, there
seems to be little or no justification (apart from an appeal to the
weight of tradition) for putting a special emphasis on the leadership role of a single ministerial group, the successors to either the
presbyters or the bishops of certain early strands in the tradition.
Moreover, on rational and experiential grounds, there are considerable arguments against it. There is no compelling reason
why an individual who is gifted in public speaking and teaching
will be equally gifted in communicating privately with individuals,
in sustaining them patiently through their unhappiness, in
mediating a healing power or in enabling others to exercise this
ministry of care. The demand that a diversity of functions related
to the life of the church must be focused in one person, the
"shepherd of the flock," must therefore appear unwise on
grounds of reason and experience. It may have been functional in
eras or cultures that lacked resources for corporate leadership,
but it hardly applies when education is widely available, when
social structures are increasingly democratic, and when people
have the freedom to discover their unique gifts for Christian
service.

An alternative approach to the relationship between pastoral
care and the ministry is one that starts with the ministry of the
whole people of God and then considers the place of pastoral care
within it. In the previous chapter I referred to H. Richard
Niebuhr's phrase, "the increase of love of God and neighbor," as a
good description of the aim of pastoral care. This aim can be
related to the life of the whole church by reference to three
reasons for the church's existence: *kerygma* (preaching), *koinōnia*
(fellowship), and *diakonia* (service).[25] As soon as any of these
functions of the church is neglected, the church loses sight of its
place in the world as the body of the crucified and risen Christ.
The three functions are each dependent upon the other. When
they are separated, preaching degenerates into self-right-
eousness, fellowship into exclusiveness, and service into unreflec-
tive activism. Thus the functions must be held together in creative
tension, but this does not mean that one individual in the congregation should try to unite them in his or her person. A blend of
these functions can be obtained only when the diversity of personality, experience, and ability in the Christian congregation *as a
whole* is allowed to attain its full richness.

Against this background we may now return to the definition of
pastoral care as the increase of love of God and neighbor. Un-
questionably this love is vitalized through preaching and sacramental worship. An ordained minister acting as the leader of
worship can nourish the whole congregation with a ministry that
is informed and passionate, both sustaining them and opening
their hearts to the needs of others. The selection and training of a
particular group of people to perform this task, on the basis of
extensive study of theology, scripture, history, and practice, leads
to an ordained ministry as we know it at present. The leader of
worship is also in a natural position to influence the *koinōnia* and
diakonia of the congregation. But here precisely the greatest
danger lies. For one person can never create and sustain fellowship and one person cannot encompass all that is implied in
Christian service.

Thus the trend of our argument does not deny the need for

leadership of the Christian congregation in the task of *diakonia* (provided, of course, this is understood in its distinctively Christ-like form as humble servanthood), but it does raise urgently the question of where such leadership should be found and of what character it should be. The following description of a provider of pastoral care suggests that the gifts and experience some "ordi-nary" members possess prepare them as well as any ordained minister for a ministry of care of others.

> Mrs. L. came to this parish twenty-five years ago with her ex-army husband and three teen-age daughters, and for the first time became an active church member. Her husband died of cancer after a difficult illness. She went through the bereavement with strength and maturity. I soon found that in the case of similar bereavements she was able to bring great comfort. Since then she has given pastoral care in many cases of illness and particularly bereavement. I may bring the "official" support of the church, but she brings the real comfort and love. She has no training or formal education but she has a down-to-earth approach and knows how to communicate sympathy in terms people can understand.

It may seem strange to describe Mrs. L.'s simple form of helping as leadership, but this is because we have become trapped in a particular form of congregational leadership, based on the image of the highly trained, verbally articulate, "professional" person. Such people may make good preachers and able administrators, but they can be unhelpful guides to others in their need to offer a ministry of love. Mrs. L. leads others by being loving in the only way she knows. Yet this way leads others out of death's darkness, and in leading them she also prepares them to lead others. The leadership of pastoral care should bring out in others also the gift of leadership when the occasion arises.

Thus the churches need to give more honor to the leadership of service and to find those who possess such gifts, encouraging them to develop their gifts and to share them with others. Fre-quently sexist attitudes have designated such humble tasks as suitable only for female "helpers," who then must be kept in a subservient role directed by the spokes*men* of the ordained ministry. But, with the ever-increasing numbers of women in the ordained ministry, such stereotyped sexual roles cannot long endure. In their place there must come equal regard for witness, fellowship, and service in the church. The talents of men and women alike should be devoted to each sphere, according to their special vocation. A theology of vocation, confident (in Lutheran style) of the sheer joy of loving one's neighbor, will discover in the church's wider membership some surprising resources for a revitalized ministry of love.

CHAPTER 3

The Professional Captivity
of
Pastoral Care

A man coming to you for help. The essential difference between
your role in this situation and his is obvious. He comes for help to
you. You don't come for help to him. . . . You are not equals and
cannot be.

> Martin Buber,
> in dialogue with
> Carl R. Rogers,
> in Buber's *The Knowledge of Man*

In the previous chapter I argued for a breaking of the link
between the ordained ministry of the church and the ministry of
pastoral care, seeking instead an approach to pastoral care that
could liberate all believers to pursue their vocation of love of God
and neighbor. But might it not still be the case that experts—even
if not ordained clergy—are required for such a task? Who is to
lead, train, and organize such a ministry? Is it not inevitable that
some kind of leadership is required?

In considering this question I wish to stress first the inherent
danger of claiming any expertise in caring. This danger is accu-
rately pinpointed in Martin Buber's response to Carl Rogers's
claim that professional psychotherapy is a form of I-Thou encounter. Buber responds, "You are not equals and cannot be." As
soon as one institutionalizes a helping role one creates inequality
between people. This may, of course, be an appropriate, useful,
and morally acceptable inequality. But it is undeniably inequality,
a quite different relationship from the free encounter between

persons that Buber is describing in his terminology of I and Thou. To offer oneself as an accredited helper is to impose limits upon the character of the relationship, to keep oneself apart in order to concentrate on the need of the other and to define the duration and depth of the encounter solely according to what the other requires in order to be helped. But is this also the true character of pastoral care as the increase of love of God and neighbor?

THE QUESTION OF EXPERTISE

A debate in the United States in the 1960s which found its counterpart in Britain in the early 1970s can help us focus on this question. In April 1963 the American Association of Pastoral Counselors (AAPC) was founded. In the preamble to the AAPC constitution a clear clerical and specialist focus was maintained:

> We recognize that in a broad sense all clergy do some pastoral counseling. The primary concern of this Association, however, is with those clergymen who, having acquired specialized training and experience, have chosen to identify themselves as specialists.[1]

The new organization set as its aims professional sharing and communication, standard-setting, certification, interfaith cooperation, interpretation (of pastoral counseling to the churches and to "allied professions"), and research. There were opponents to the founding of the association, most notably Seward Hiltner, who expressed his misgivings in an article in *Pastoral Psychology* to which Howard Clinebell, the chairman of the new association, responded.[2] Hiltner's main concern was that a rift would develop between the specialism of pastoral counseling and the churches, and he saw the establishment of a hierarchy of counselor grades and the endorsement of fees for private practice as evidence that the ordinary Christian fellowship was being bypassed. In his reply Howard Clinebell admitted that there were dangers, including the danger of loss of connection with the local church, but he argued that these could be overcome and that, in any case, there was an urgent need to introduce standards and controls in view of the dramatic expansion of pastoral counseling centers, some of dubious standing.

It is interesting, looking at this debate from the vantage point of twenty years later, to note the points over which Hiltner and Clinebell do *not* disagree. Both writers take it for granted that the emergence and consolidation of expertise in pastoral counseling is unequivocally a good development. Neither writer finds it necessary to explore the relationship of pastoral counseling to pastoral care, and both equate pastoral counseling with counseling by ordained clergy. Thus the issues of professionalism and clericalism are simply not raised; expertise is equated with excellence; and it is assumed that there is a straightforward connection between professional counseling and Christian caring.

A very different set of questions arises from the debate provoked in Britain in 1971 by proposals to establish a national pastoral organization.[3] In the forefront of the debate was the late R. A. Lambourne, who was both a doctor and a theologian. He wrote a position paper entitled "Objections to a National Pastoral Organization,"[4] which raised fundamental theological and sociological questions about accreditation and standardization in pastoral care and counseling. The flavor of Lambourne's argument can be sensed in his description of the character of pastoral care as "a pattern of corporate responsible sensitive acts motivated by a compelling vision."[5] This starting point leads Lambourne to oppose increasing in the pastoral care field the kind of professionalism already evident in medicine or social work. Instead, he claims, we should see pastoral care as "lay, voluntary and diffuse in the community" and "motivated as much by a struggle for corporate excellence as a struggle against defects."[6] (We might rephrase this statement of Lambourne's in terms introduced in the previous chapter by saying that he wishes to reassert the *koinōnia* element in pastoral care.) In order to maintain the lay, diffuse, adventurous, and variegated aspects of pastoral care Lambourne suggests that far more attention should be paid to the tasks of creating a healthy interpersonal life, which would be concerned less with the eradication of individual problems and defects and more with the enhancement of values through worship, social action, and "mutual confrontation and confirmation." If training was to be developed it should concentrate on models of the ordinary and communal, not the specialized and institutional. Thus hospital settings and the structured psychotherapeutic interview were seen as quite inappropriate models for the pastoral care of the future. According to Lambourne the aim should be the development of a wide variety of experimental courses in lay training and education, not the creation of a counseling elite within the church.

As an international figure in the pastoral counseling field Howard Clinebell found himself once more in the role of respondent to criticisms of specialization in pastoral counseling. In his response to Lambourne[7] Clinebell wholeheartedly sided with his statement of goals and shared his fears about adopting false models of pastoral care and institutionalizing the outmoded. Nevertheless, he parted company with Lambourne over the question of professionalization in pastoral care and over the heavy emphasis Lambourne put on growth at the expense of healing. Clinebell argued that Lambourne was creating a false dichotomy between lay and professional. He expressed his own view as follows:

> In our complex society, it is the complementarity of the lay and the professional dimensions which makes pastoral care viable. Well-trained professionals can provide the essential training of the laity that will release their potentialities for caring ministries. A one-sided emphasis on the lay character of pastoral care, without a parallel emphasis on the role of competent professionals, can lead to the dangers of inadequately trained and coached lay shepherds.[8]

In the remainder of his article Clinebell offered a list of skills which might be included in training so that the corporate aspects of ministry could be enhanced. Thus he reiterated the need for standards and accreditation, but altered the content toward which such standardization would be geared.

We see that despite Clinebell's appreciative comments, the difference in outlook between him and Lambourne is in reality quite profound. For Clinebell the notion of expertise remains normative; for Lambourne it is precisely the use of this norm that creates the danger. Clinebell wants the expert to teach the laity; Lambourne wants to mobilize the laity so that they can challenge the narrowness of vision of the experts. Despite his interest in growth models, Clinebell sees pastoral care primarily as a problem-solving activity: Lambourne wishes to change it into a mutual search for excellence, with no acknowledged experts on the route. In the last analysis, the difference may be seen as that between a writer who views *care* from the perspective of *counseling* and one who views *counseling* from the perspective of *care*. Inevitably the center of attention is very different in each case.

PROFESSIONALISM AND CAPTIVITY

The strengths in Clinebell's approach will be emphasized at a later stage, but first we can tease out in greater detail Lambourne's critique of the professional model. As I have argued elsewhere,[9] an overstress on competence in counseling skills may result in a loss of the transcendent dimension of pastoral care, which is to be found in the depths of the helper and the helped alike. Thus professionalism may be regarded as a kind of captivity, shutting away both helper and helped from the full possibilities of care. This captivity has various features: lack of mutuality, maldistribution of influence and power, intellectualism, neglect of the communal dimension, and resistance to radical change.

Lack of Mutuality

If we consider once more Buber's comment about the relationship between therapist and client we shall confront the major problem of emphasizing counseling expertise in pastoral care: "You are not equals and cannot be." It might seem that the development of highly sophisticated counseling techniques has produced resources to cope with this problem. Any trained counselor has learned to discern the difference between appropriate and inappropriate dependence, to avoid the dangers of countertransference, and to shift the therapeutic interaction (at the appropriate stage) from a "parent-child" to an "adult-adult" level. Yet such sophistication can also mask the deeper levels of the problem as far as pastoral care and counseling is concerned. This deeper level concerns the claim to expertise (and therefore to inequality) that the counseling relationship itself enshrines. Counseling precludes mutuality. We may come to grips with this issue by means of the following lengthy case illustration:

Andrea was forty-seven when her husband died suddenly and without warning. Although she had received no formal education since school she was an intelligent and thoughtful person. She had devoted herself to her husband's life and work—both his private business and public service. As a mother she had brought her children up to be quickly independent, and when her husband died she was traumatically on her own. In the early weeks and months of grief Andrea was reasonably supported by family and friends. There seemed to be little need of professional help apart from routine visits from the minister and the doctor.

Soon after the first anniversary of her husband's death, Andrea's friends started to tire of her incessant talk about him. Clearly they could not, and would not, recognize Andrea's natural need to talk in this way. Gradually she became isolated from others and her overwhelming sense of loneliness and loss of status intensified. To counteract this she flung herself into various forms of voluntary service, in the course of which she found a new friend, hitherto unknown, who happened to be a social worker with a particular interest in grief and bereavement.

It transpired later that the social worker's initial response to Andrea was not overt friendship, but covert professional interest in observing the grief process. Brigit, the social worker, became increasingly concerned at Andrea's loneliness and began to feel increasingly unable to help. Soon thoughts of Andrea began to dominate Brigit's mind and evoked in her a range of difficult and negative emotions including guilt and anxiety.

One evening after a meeting of the voluntary group to which they both belonged Andrea invited Brigit home for coffee. Brigit felt particularly tense, strangely excited, and found difficulty in keeping her own feelings in check. As Andrea yet again shared her utter sense of loneliness and her conviction that there was no way through, Brigit became increasingly emotional with a deepening sense of abject failure. She was about to go when Andrea seemed to indicate that she recognized Brigit's need to talk. Somehow Andrea had created an atmosphere in which it was safe for Brigit to express her feelings with an uninhibited freedom.

During the course of the next two hours Brigit told Andrea of her failure, as she saw it, to respond to her dying mother's need. Brigit's mother had died seven years before. Throughout the night before she died, though Brigit had been in the room, she had not been at her bedside and had not wanted to "be with" her mother in any real sense. Since then, Brigit had found herself unable to share this experience. Without recognizing the significance in personal terms, she had developed a keen academic interest in grief and bereavement. Now, when faced with another person's grief, Brigit's failure with her mother was heightened and replicated by her sense of failure with Andrea. In the month that followed this incident Andrea and Brigit's friendship developed. Together they recognized the vital necessity of creating between them an atmosphere of complete openness and trust in which "anything could be said or told." Through this friendship a major change occurred for each person. Brigit found an ability to integrate herself—the bad with the good—the failures with the successes. As a result she related more effectively to her clients by being more "at peace" in herself.

The fascination of the story of Andrea and Brigit is the way in which personal friendship and professional concern intertwine. Brigit saw herself for a time as Andrea's helper (counselor even) as well as her friend, but healing at depth occurred only when Brigit's need also became apparent and Andrea was set free to *give* as well as to receive care.

Here we see the essential difficulty in using the counseling relationship as a paradigm for pastoral care. The whole activity of counseling depends on certain ground rules which determine the respective positions of helper and helped. No counseling technique, however egalitarian or antipaternalistic in character, can enable the counselor to step outside the rules and still claim to be a counselor. The relationship is—and must be for the protection of both parties— one of inequality, in which the counselor controls the situation with the client's agreement. This is the great strength of counseling, since it makes the services of one skilled person available to many without raising the unrealistic expectation that each counseling encounter will be an act of personal friendship. But if pastoral care is essentially the nurturing of love of God and neighbor, then the pastoral counseling paradigm must take a very minor place within it. In its place must come the more demanding and risky activity of love without the protection of designated helping roles—love in the unstructured world outside the counseling context, where all are struggling and none can offer or receive the comfort of expertise. It is in this world that the lives of most Christians are spent and that they are called to the ministry of pastoral care, ill-equipped if not defenseless. Thus pastoral care must be freed from the captivity of expertise in counseling.

Maldistribution of Influence and Power

Still more alien to the spirit of pastoral care is the tendency for professionals to perpetrate, or even increase, social inequality. T. J. Johnson has pointed out in *Professions and Power* that the following conditions promote the accumulation of power by a professional group: an element of uncertainty in what is provided by the professional; a large, heterogeneous and vulnerable client group; a relationship initiated by the client but terminated by the judgment of the professional.[10] Such conditions have led to the high income, social prestige, and negotiating power of the two most "successful" modern professions—medicine and law. It is just such conditions that lead to the rise and perpetuation of the "counseling professions."

If the professional counseling model is too easily applied to pastoral care it will lead rapidly to what may be described as a "middle-class captivity." Certainly there is little prestige, power, or income in becoming an acknowledged pastoral expert, but power of a more subtle kind is accumulated. The groups in society who are articulate, better educated, more accustomed to dealing with other professional groups as equals dominate the helping roles in the church, while the simpler person struggling to cope with problems unknown to the middle-class group becomes the perpetual occupant of the client position. Thus by professionalizing pastoral care we fall into the grave danger of perpetuating the dominance of middle-class attitudes towards the church's ministry of care within society. This aspect of the captivity of pastoral care is a subtle trap from which escape is very difficult. Since people who reflect upon and write about pastoral care are themselves articulate, educated, and middle-class (I include myself), it is almost impossible for them to imagine alternative approaches. Yet if the captivity is not overcome, pastoral care is in danger of being yet another device for ensuring that the "haves" continue to hold power over the "have-nots" and that the insights of the poor and lowly are lost.

Intellectualism

Related to this difficulty is the connection between professional practice and intellectual ability which is enshrined in the professional ideal. It is no accident that the most ancient professional groups have been categorized as the "learned professions." Quite central to the notion of professional expertise is the grasp of a large and intellectually complex body of special knowledge. Entry to professions in modern times is determined to a large extent by intellectual capacity, and the most common cause of failure to attain professional status is lack of academic success, not lack of appropriate personal attributes. This highly intellectualist approach inevitably influences all methods of pastoral care that stress professionalism. It is true, certainly, that the Clinical Pastoral Education movement has been at pains to counterbalance intellectualism with a stress on learning by doing and emotional growth. Nevertheless, the professional, however practical, however emotionally tuned, remains the one who knows the special language, who can verbalize feelings and apply theoretical categories to the situations he or she encounters. But such intellectual abilities do not necessarily help in the Christian ministry of love. If we use professional specialized knowledge as an ideal for all, we fall into an ancient error—that only those who *know* can love God and neighbor. Then pastoral care becomes the captive of gnostic heresy. The simplicity of faith is overcome by the complexity of knowledge.

Neglect of Communal Dimension

The main brunt of Lambourne's attack on accreditation in pastoral care was directed at the individualism implicit in the professional relationship. We have noted earlier that trustworthiness is seen to be central to this relationship. This implies a trust by the client that his or her welfare is the sole concern of the practitioner. This commitment is expressed well in the Geneva Convention Code of Medical Ethics: "The health of my patient will be my first consideration." The use of the possessive "my" is most significant here. The doctor enters into a direct relationship with each individual patient, taking on a quite specific and personal responsibility. Herein lies the effectiveness of person-centered professional care, but it is precisely this effectiveness that creates difficulties for professionals in the social and political arena. The issue has emerged most plainly in social work with the rise of the radical social work movement, which has questioned the morality of tending for individual clients while ignoring the destructive features of society that create many of their problems.[11] Similarly, medical and nursing care, while gaining great sophistication and skill in individual treatment, have not had the same success in influencing political priorities in health care provision or social attitudes toward preventive health care measures. The intensity of the one-to-one encounters of professional practice appears to create a blind spot with respect to the sociopolitical context of care.

Thus the problem that the professional model creates for pastoral care has serious ethical dimensions. Pastoral care can never be concerned solely with the adjustment of the individual or with the promotion of personal fulfillment. The moral context of pastoral care[12] implies challenge to the lifestyle of both the individual and the social group. The "safe anonymity" of the consulting room is not the normal arena for pastoral care. Rather, the arena is the heat and dust of daily life, where destructive forces crush the weak and where whole groups of individuals suffer injustice or the loss of all hope. In another article,[13] Lambourne has described the dangerous "love affair" between pastoral counseling and psychotherapy and has suggested that the prophetic edge of pastoral work is being dulled by that liaison. This assertion is not easily proved or disproved, but certainly it does seem to be the case that urban renewal, minority rights, peace movements, and other moral concerns espoused by Christians have not found any place in the dominant "clinical" model of pastoral care.[14] The pastoral and the moral have been isolated in separate worlds, with little interaction at the intellectual or the practical level. But if pastoral care is to face up to the issue of the *koinōnia* of Christians and the relationship of that *koinōnia* to the wider society, then issues of personal and social morality inevitably arise.

Resistance to Radical Social Change

Finally, professionalism is not only individualistic, it is also change-resistant, conservative of existing social structures. This would appear to be an inevitable aspect of professionalism by virtue of the social dynamics that lead to its emergence. The social context of the modern notion of the professional expert is that of the transformation of traditional society into the vast, rapidly changing, and relatively insecure social groupings of postindustrial society. Professionals fulfill in modern society functions that would have been undertaken in the past by family or by respected figures within a small social group. They can maintain this position only by presenting a relatively united front to the public they serve. Thus collegial control is essential, so that the professional group can retain autonomy, rather than be subject to the kind of political changes that might weaken their position. This means that professional groups are rarely willing to expose to public view the relativity and uncertainty of their own expertise. While prophetic members of professions do arise from time to time, their calls for the radical revision of education or health care or legal practice are silenced or at least muted by their colleagues concerned with maintaining a status quo that brings them security.

Here then is the most insidious captivity of pastoral care, for institutions once successfully established do not readily reform themselves. The more people gain a secure and satisfying occupation in being accredited pastoral counselors, the less easy it will be for them to question the whole basis of their position. Yet humility, insecurity, and vulnerability are at the heart of pastoral care, if it is a following of the ministry of Jesus. It becomes hard to see how professional associations (described by the British social scientist Richard Titmuss as "associations for spreading the gospel of self-importance"[15]) can cohabit with a care that knows none of the security of the socially successful. It would be a healthier position for pastoral care if "experts" were the pariahs rather than the culture heroes and heroines of modern society.

ESCAPE FROM CAPTIVITY

But must professionalism be merely the dark and airless prison I have been describing? What would freedom from such a prison be like for those countless Christians who might offer pastoral care in their daily lives? Here we must consider carefully the nature of freedom. The philosopher Immanuel Kant quotes a saying about the dove, which, feeling the resistance of the air against its wings, might suppose that without such an obstacle it could fly more freely. But, of course, the resistance is necessary for the flight. The same must be said for freedom. Freedom is not the denial of all structure, the absence of all constraint. Rather it is the use of appropriate structure to attain the goals we have chosen. Certainly we must not abandon pastoral care to the chaos of undisciplined and unexamined "common sense." Much injury is done in the name of a common sense that is merely prejudice disguised as simplicity. The true simplicity of pastoral care does not come easily, and for most of us it is not a natural aptitude that we can apply without preparation, discipline, and careful thought.

Thus we must replace the alien captivity of a narrowly conceived professionalism with structures of a different quality. These are structures that challenge our prejudices and prepare us for action in a world where all human institutions share in the distortions of sin. We are taken back to the root of professionalism—*professio,* a public declaration of intent. In considering such structures for pastoral care we shall have to remind ourselves what it is that pastoral care intends to achieve. The following example may help us begin this task:

> George will soon be ninety. A widower living alone in a two-room apartment, he exists in unbelievable squalor. The stench is almost unbearable. He is mentally sound, and determined to stay on.
>
> The whole phalanx of social welfare is out to help—to no avail. An excellent doctor calls every three weeks. George has had "meals on wheels," which he rejects. He has had a "home-help," whom he accused of stealing because he wanted to get rid of her.
>
> His next of kin, a cousin by marriage, visits every day and is in danger of a breakdown. "Can the church do something?" I contacted the local old people's home, filled out forms, obtained his signature (all the time *knowing* he would renege!). And when a place was offered he refused to go.
>
> So how best to help? How to create minimum conditions of hygiene? How to help neighbors to accept? How to encourage next of kin *not* to go in every day? How to help George know that he's not a naughty boy, but a friendly and interesting old man entitled to his privacy and even isolation?

It is clear that pastoral care of George cannot consist in mobilizing yet another of the social services that he so stalwartly rejects, nor does it seem convincing to say that George needs a skilled counselor, unless counseling is understood in a very broad sense. George does not appear to lack insight into his situation. He knows what he wants and he makes it perfectly plain to any who seek to advise him. The problem is that what he wants is creating severe difficulties for those around him. But George is not a problem to be "managed." He is a person to be loved, truly loved on his terms. That is the task of pastoral care.

It is from the elements of such a love that we may construct an appropriate "structure of freedom" for pastoral care. The first requirement is that love be physical. George's smelly condition puts all who would help him to the test! But love crosses the barriers of our natural reactions, allowing us to touch, embrace, or stay beside those whose condition or deformity makes them repulsive in others' eyes. It cannot be, then, that the true profession of pastoral care is to be learned in the aseptic conditions of the counselor's office, but never in the dirt and stench of the hidden wildernesses of the affluent society. (Here lies the greatest danger in the dominance of the middle-class counseling model.)

Second, love requires an understanding of George on his own terms. Here he is at the end of a journey. Who will share the last resting with him and look back with him to the route he has taken? George cannot be loved by the person who merely understands his "syndrome," namely the "disengagement" of the elderly, which is often expressed in hostility and defensiveness. Theories are useful when you wish to deal with someone routinely in order to accommodate them to a social system. But love loves not theory but story. Love enters the particular situation and lives in it for a while, sharing with the other at levels that the intellect cannot entertain. By sharing in another's story one is "being with" rather than "doing to."

Third, George and those around him must be *confronted* by love. Love can be hard. It seeks out goodness and truth, and cannot accept compromise, if that entails the destruction of human value. George's situation cannot merely be accepted.

Someone must show him the pain he is causing to his cousin and to those conscientious helpers who are constantly running a-ground on his stubbornness. And someone must also ask what the social isolation of people like George says about the character of modern society.

Thus from love may emerge some structures that liberate pastoral care for its true profession. We have seen that love entails a discipline of the physical, bringing care in contact and closeness; that it seeks story rather than theory in order to create a companionship with others; and that it requires a passion for honesty and truth in both personal and societal dimensions. In the next chapter we shall consider what such structures might mean in practical terms, in order to create a distinctive professionalism in pastoral care—but also to transcend all expertise and to go beyond every form of professionalism.

CHAPTER 4

Professionalism
and
Beyond

"Look here," Furii said, "I never promised you a rose garden. I
never promised you perfect justice. . . . I never promised lies, and
the rose-garden world of perfection is a lie—and a bore too!"

Hannah Green,
I Never Promised You a Rose Garden

If certain styles of professionalism can become a form of captivity for pastoral care, then we must pay the greatest attention to the
alternatives that might be proposed. Liberation from one captivity could well mean enslavement in a much worse one. We must
first realize that to oppose the wrong kind of professionalism in
pastoral care is not to sweep aside everything that has been
achieved through the training of clergy in counseling and relationship skills by methods developed in the Clinical Pastoral Education movement. This might appear to be an implication of my
argument in the last two chapters. But, in fact, the purpose of that
argument was solely to prevent specialized counseling by clergy
becoming *normative* for pastoral care. Such specialism must be
given its appropriate place in the overall scheme for the increase
of the gospel of love in the world. This place is a relatively minor
one compared with the task that confronts *every* Christian who
seeks to be true to his or her vocation. So the alternative professionalism we seek must be one that enhances everyday caring by
giving it a framework for consistency and a vision for development.

The first essential characteristic of an alternative professionalism in pastoral care is that it takes with total seriousness the
reality and pervasiveness of sin. In Hannah Green's novel, *I Never
Promised You a Rose Garden,* a young schizophrenic girl, Deborah,
is brought painfully and patiently through her illness by a
psychotherapist to whom she gives the code name Furii.[1] The
words of Furii at the head of this chapter—"I never promised you
a rose garden"—speak volumes about truth in caring. In a world
torn by war, racial conflict, economic injustice, and nuclear madness there can be no honesty in utopian promises for personal
fulfillment. The help any person offers to another must often
appear to be a tiny oasis of love in a desert of selfishness and
greed. T.S. Eliot's bitter words in *The Waste Land* describe such a
desert well:

> A heap of broken images, where the sun beats,
> And the dead tree gives no shelter, the cricket no relief,
> And the dry stone no sound of water.[2]

Thus we do injustice to our fellow humans, caught in the despair
of a world without hope and without shelter from cruelty, if we
promise them "a rose garden." Genuine care, in the context of the
Christian gospel, means feeling at least some of the weight of the
cross of sin that oppresses others. Pastoral care demands a radical
questioning of easy solutions to the human condition. In Dietrich
Bonhoeffer's memorable phrases, it questions "cheap grace" and
knows the "cost of discipleship."[3]

We saw already in the previous chapter the beginnings of a
framework for the kind of alternative professionalism required
for pastoral care, which would be grounded in a realistic and
radical love. Three features were noted: the discipline of the
physical, story in place of theory, and the quest for truth. I shall
now build upon this framework by considering, first, how such an
approach can be described as "professional," second, how it re-
lates to the nature and tasks of the church, and finally how it
might inform our understanding of specific pastoral situations.

THE REVALUATION OF
PROFESSIONALISM

I have already rejected the idea that professionalism in pastoral care should be equated with pastoral care by ordained clergy (see chap. 2), but this does not imply that the knowledge, skill, responsibility, and commitment associated with professionalism should be totally swept aside. To the extent that professionalism is more than merely a monopolistic claim to status and power, its public declaration of intent is based upon serious and verifiable efforts to provide consistent and effective service to others. The professed intent of the Christian community is to love one another and to promote the gospel of love throughout the world. A pastoral care that seeks to honor this intent must demonstrate the seriousness of its commitment. It cannot depend upon mere impulses of the moment or upon a naive faith in the good will of ordinary folk. The task of loving is both complex and demanding. It requires study and prayerful preparation. It cannot be achieved by the person who fears pain and insecurity. Above all, it requires the discipline of self-examination and honest criticism of others. All those features that make professionalism a *genuine* claim to efficacy are required by a pastoral care that means what it says. Declarations of intent and exhortations to love are of no use if they are not implemented in quite specific, practical, and consistent ways of acting.

We can see more clearly the character of this professionalism if we consider once more the "impossible possibility" of the demand to love. The following story illustrates how easily well-meaning ministers and church members can find themselves caught in the web of others' problems and be put in a position where love seems tested to the breaking point:

Muriel is a woman in her mid-forties, who has developed a "difficult" personality along with multiple handicaps, for example, epilepsy, education in a "special" school, rejection, arthritis of the hip, deafness. Nevertheless she has maintained apparent independence, living in a women's hostel, working at a live-in waitress job, and now living in sheltered housing. She has on-off relationships with a sister in the city and a brother who lives some distance away. She alternately loves and hates them. She has acquired a good medical vocabulary and takes a strange pleasure in playing off the many doctors and consultants who have cared for her. Recently she has responded to loneliness by attention-seeking gestures—falling in the fire and receiving third-degree burns, breaking her house windows with her head, threatening suicide. When she lived in the center of the city she joined by adult baptism the local Baptist church, which, thanks to a member with a large car, she has continued to attend from a much greater distance. So the minister and several church people are also involved in her pastoral care, by telephone, visit, and in church, where some are quite upset by her oddity and evident discomfort as she is helped into her wheelchair. The local church has offered pastoral care and she has accepted visits ungraciously.

So what do we do? The professionals have case conferences, without inviting the minister or any of the church people concerned with her, and confess themselves worn and baffled. The church alternates between feeling pleased that such an unhappy person should seek solace and be faithful to it over a period of eight years, and a feeling of frustration, annoyance, and embarrassment. In her most alarming moods, or her times of most extravagant acting-out, Bible reading and prayer seem to calm her for a time. The church seems to be the one institution to which she gives money and from which she receives nothing tangible—so we continue to be there—willing to talk to and consult other caring agents, but wondering what will happen next to Muriel and to us!

The kind of professionalism required of the Christian fellowship from which Muriel seeks help is very different from that which could be offered by any other group. She may receive some therapy and support from medical or social work agencies, but the need she feels is deeper and more demanding than anything such services can meet. We might say that her need is a "spiritual" one, provided that that much-abused word is not misunderstood. Her physical disabilities and her disturbed personality make her a stranger in human society, someone who cannot easily fit into the style of modern living, with its demands for conformity, reasonableness, and predictability. Muriel may be helped by the personal attention of a minister or priest, perhaps especially one who has acquired specific counseling skills, but, eventually, it is to the Christian congregation as a whole that she presents the greatest challenge. Can people like her be given a place in the Christian fellowship? If the fellowship of those who profess love cannot accept her, then she is an alien indeed. That is why her problem is in the last analysis a spiritual one. Like the many lost and frightened people whom Jesus encountered in his ministry, she seeks and yet often sabotages the healing touch of unembarrassed and freely given love. She shows in her person how hard it is to find from others a love that seeks not comfort or reward, but wants only to give. She needs someone to come alongside her and stay with her in her strangeness.

Thus it is through the heightening of the capacity to know and to express love that the Christian becomes a "professional" in pastoral care. This entails the whole complexity of love from its bodily and emotional expressions to its mysterious and transcendent character. A disembodied love is not the answer, nor is the elevation of the physical to a false importance. The ideal that is sought is a union of body and spirit, where physical gesture and bodily contact are at one with the relationship needs of the other. There is a flow in self-giving love, reminiscent perhaps of the richness of true worship of God, where body, mind, and spirit complement each other in the act of helping. Yet so many barriers stand in the way of such a unified love that Christians are more often aware of their sinfulness, selfishness, and failures to love than they are of the gift of love which is their privilege to receive and pass joyfully to others. The whole discipline of the Christian life—Bible-reading, self-examination, private prayer and public worship, fellowship building and prophetic action—can be seen as a response to this awareness of sin. Christians cannot claim to have any expertise in love or any final knowledge of its mysterious power to heal and save. But they are the ones who "turn again," who recognize the fragmentation of physical desire, friendship, and an all-embracing love within themselves, and who seek God's help to give to others what they alone cannot give. In this determined and disciplined "turning again" lies the professionalism of all pastoral care.

WITNESS, COMMUNITY, AND SERVICE

The context of this discipline of love is the church. This is an aspect of the distinctiveness of pastoral care, which makes the description "professional" only partially appropriate. There is nothing in the secular professions of medicine, law, nursing, or social work that corresponds with the concept of the church as both the locus and the source of pastoral care. Most professional groups see themselves as having two, or possibly three, directions of responsibility: responsibility to clients, responsibility to colleagues, and, possibly, responsibility to an employing authority or to the society that licenses them.[4] Thus there are, for such groups, *separate* though overlapping areas of responsibility, and frequently the collegial responsibility is seen as the most important, since this ensures the autonomy and strength of a distinctive professional approach.

The context of pastoral care, on the other hand, is much more ambiguous in character. Pastoral care is exercised both *within* and *by* the church, which is the body of Christ, a fallible and weak body attempting to continue his ministry in a "time between the times." This body is undeniably within the world and it shares in all the relativities and uncertainties of earthly existence. Yet, at the same time, the body that is fully *in* this world is warned not to be *of* this world. It possesses a higher loyalty than any the world can command. Such a position effectively prevents pastoral care from being reduced to activities that might lessen the pain and contradiction of being the body of Christ.

In the first place, there is always the tendency for pastoral care to become merely a form of chaplaincy to the religiously committed. Images of shepherds, flocks, and sheepfolds are used to suggest that a small community of believers is to be tended in a safe refuge far from the harshness of the world outside. Such a view effectively creates professional pastors, selected by the churches to ensure the safety and good order of the Christian community through the turbulence of social changes and the uncertainties of earthly life. If this were the only context of pastoral care, then certainly an ordained ministry, in an analogy with other professional groups, will be likely to exercise such care effectively. Authorized training procedures, collegial supervision, and responsibility to the institution can ensure that the "flock" is guarded, nourished, and led with authority. But where, when this is the dominant model for pastoral care, is to be found the diversity, growth, and *vulnerability* of the body of Christ?

At an opposite extreme, pastoral care may become detached from its locus in the Christian community and establish itself as a separate activity within the society at large. This would appear to be a common development when specialist counseling services are developed under church auspices. As the debate about the formation of the American Association of Pastoral Counselors demonstrated (see chap. 3), the specialism of pastoral counseling is in danger of having a merely nominal attachment to the local church and of breaking away from its theological roots. When this happens, it is again quite easy to describe professionalism in pastoral care, but it is one in which answerability to specialist colleagues is paramount, and in which standards drawn from other professional counseling groups become normative. Such developments may well increase the quality of care within the society at large, but they do not assist the Christian community to exercise its distinctive ministry of care.

Between these extremes there lies the uncertain and vulnerable position of attempting to remain under the headship of Christ and to obey his command to "go out into all the world" (Matt. 28:19–20). This is not to be seen as a commission for a narrowly and dogmatically conceived evangelism. Rather, it is a sharing of the gifts of discipleship, joyfully and with no thought of superior-ity. Pastoral care dissolves the boundary between the church and the world, since it mediates a love that knows no bounds. It is the opening of the body to the world, with all the danger of hurt that that implies, so that what is good within it may be shared by others.

Thus the context of pastoral care is neither the Christian community exclusively, nor merely the society within which that community is established. There must be a restlessness about too great a commitment to either Christian institutions or secular institutions, since ultimately the body of Christ belongs to neither. The fragility of that context for pastoral care is often lost, since few of us can tolerate for long too great an ambiguity in our sources of value and guidance. But to seek a haven in secular counseling values or in the false certainties of a church that denies its weakness and failures is to lose the path where Christ's body journeys. Only a living, and therefore a changing, growing, and vulnerable, body can find that path.

We return, then, to the necessity to relate pastoral care to the whole life of the church in witness (*kerygma*), fellowship (*koinōnia*), and service (*diakonia*). These three terms make it plain that there can be no radical division between the church and the world, and that a diversity of gifts is called for if the church is to fulfill, even in the slightest degree, its function as Christ's body. All three functions have an inward and an outward aspect. A church that cannot hear the Word itself has no way of speaking to others; a community that knows no love within its constituent parts has only the acid of resentment to spread outside; and people who find no joy in giving or receiving care from another will have nothing to offer but their pride and self-sufficiency. So the life of a church that knows how to listen, love, and serve should spill over into the world through the daily lives of Christians; and the pains of that world, felt in those daily lives, should never cease to challenge the church to a more costly discipleship. Out of this dynamic a rich form of caring can be created, one that does not depend upon a specialist group, but that mirrors the life of the whole church as a witnessing, loving, and serving community.

THE IMPLEMENTATION OF
PASTORAL CARE

Up to this point my descriptions of the distinctive character of pastoral care have remained at a general level, setting in a theological context the "professionalism" required. Now we may look at some of the practical implications of this approach by suggesting how the threefold structure outlined in the previous chapter might relate to specific situations of need. These suggestions are necessarily somewhat brief and incomplete, but they are intended to indicate a style of caring that will be accessible to all Christians whatever their position within the church. It is only upon such a foundation that specialist pastoral ministries should be developed.

The Discipline of Bodily Caring

Love, as we know it in this world, is love mediated by bodies. We receive love through the sound of a voice, the expression of face and eyes, the warm closeness of another body, the comfort and the stimulus of touch. This source of love is both one of the most potentially helpful and the most potentially destructive aspects of pastoral ministry, for the body has power to respect or to humiliate, to liberate or to exploit, to enrapture or to seduce, to purify or to corrupt. Such is the potency of our physical nature that it has often been an object of fear, if not disgust, within the Christian tradition. Things carnal have been seen as the antithesis of things spiritual, and sexuality, even within the boundaries of marriage, has been regarded as more of a brutal necessity than an aspect of our God-given nature. Yet without the body one is literally no-body. Our whole awareness of self and of world comes within the body, and all our knowledge is "carnal" knowledge, in the sense that fleshly receptors are required for every item of information we receive and interpret throughout our lives.

Physical presence and physical contact are thus the basic mediators of the ministry of love, and those who fear the dangers of such physicality have the greatest difficulty in participating in that ministry. They cannot learn appropriate bodily behavior until they have learned to face their fears of closeness. Here an analogy may be drawn with the association of word and sacrament in Christian worship. There can be no sacrament of Baptism without the physical effect of water on the skin and no sacrament of Communion without the taste and texture of bread and wine. The words uttered in sacramental worship have meaning only in relation to the physical events. Neither words nor physical elements possess a significance in themselves. It is in their union that the sacrament becomes a mediation of God's presence and power. In a similar way, the love that permeates a Christian fellowship and overflows into daily living is intimately related to the physical reality of the people—old and young, male and female, well and sick, strong and weak—who make up that community. Their bodily presence together in a shared space is essential to the fellowship, not some accidental and irrelevant feature of it.

The difficulty, however, is to know how to care for others in a way that avoids the alienating, demeaning, and exploitative elements of bodily closeness. This can be seen most obviously in the ambiguous relationships that can develop in counseling situations.

Stella was widowed at age thirty-three by the suicide of her husband. There are two children of the marriage, a boy and a girl, who were five and three at the time of their father's death. The marriage had been a satisfactory one, notwithstanding the husband's periods of clinical depression. The children were the product of the husband's desire to be a father. Stella claims no maternal instinct, and feels only a biological bond with them. During the last critical months of the first pregnancy the husband was an in-patient receiving psychiatric treatment for depression.

Stella was herself a late child, and is concerned about the condition of her parents, who were eighty-one and eighty-five at the time of Stella's husband's death. Her parents-in-law have distanced themselves from her. Father-in-law is a remote man, and mother-in-law has a long history of neurosis. Following the funeral, her comment to the officiating clergyman was, "Stella has merely lost a husband, but I have lost a son."

Stella claims no religious conviction, although God is real to her when she is angry, and she rails against him. Her period of mourning has been long and, at times, acute. She finds it difficult to allow expression of feelings and tries to discipline them by the intrusion of her sharp, rational faculties. The key to the protracted bereavement lies partly in the sadism of her husband's suicide, together with the multiple emotional deprivations of her early and teen-age life. Stella has retained close friendships with friends from student days, who also knew her husband, with friends made during the course of the eleven-year marriage, and with neighbors. Only one couple rejected her after the funeral—the only couple in her circle of friends with pretensions to religious commitment—he, an elder of the church, and she, a Sunday school teacher.

Stella claims that her apparent liveliness in relationship with friends is a pretense, a facade, and she feels it necessary to bury her hurt. In social situations she presents a great deal of spontaneity, partly because her wit and her faculty for relationship are largely cerebral. She presents little evidence of the deep feeling she has for other people. Her case presents the necessity for a professional approach to pastoral involvement. Because of her physical attractiveness and her deep need to be understood, she is frequently seductive. Her unmet needs have to be taken into account, as indeed do the blurred boundaries of the multiple family relationships. Stella herself carries many of the reactions that the parental systems have denied in the mourning process. It would be very easy for the nonprofessional to be sucked into her desperate, needy world.

Stella's series of traumatic experiences have made her especially vulnerable, as the writer of this case report observes. Her intellectual sharpness and her many encounters with loss make physical presence both especially alluring and especially threatening for her. Her answer is a seductiveness that will not reveal the true depth of her needs, since sexual games effectively conceal a basic need for closeness and dependable presence.

The discipline of pastoral care is not to be found in denying the presence of such sexuality but in gaining the wisdom and the courage to discern its true meaning. This cannot happen so long as sexuality remains a forbidden topic in Christian groups or so long as it is discussed only within the context of marital sexual relationships. A sacramental understanding of pastoral care can view the senses as gifts, not merely as dangerous distractions, and so help people to learn a language of the body that communicates respect and frees the other from fear. This language is a feature of every relationship from the most intimate to the most formal, though we often deny its presence. Thus sexual exploitation is often practiced merely through verbal attack and insinuation, while a bodily closeness, which in other contexts would be selfishly exploitative, can, through purity of motive, be healing and redemptive. The key lies in the quality of the love that is offered, not in the nature of the physical acts.

Pastoral care, therefore, is, and must be, physical in order to be a mediation of the gospel of love. No doubt this is a risky area, where self-examination and the guidance of fellow Christians are constantly required. It is demanding too much to expect that people will never have mixed motives or merely selfish goals in offering a physical presence. Yet the answer cannot be to shun the body. If Christians cannot risk the ambiguity of embodied love, they cannot know or share the pain and the glory that comes from following the incarnate Lord. Unlike the safe detachment of most professional care, pastoral care must struggle to redeem love in a way that risks the self for the other's sake.

Sharing the Story

A second cardinal feature of pastoral care is its willingness to "waste time" by abandoning the shortcuts of theoretical explanations. This, above all, is why models derived from other areas of care fit pastoral care so badly. If there are only a few trained experts in a given specialty, then it becomes essential to structure their involvement with clients in a way that maximizes their usefulness for as wide a population as possible. From this requirement there develops an approach based on case histories, standardized records, fixed allocations of time, and an appointment system. It is clear that this structured approach is of benefit also to the individual client, not merely to the whole population, since it helps focus the problem and prevents an undue dependence upon professional help. Structure improves both the quantity and the quality of the care available.

It is questionable, however, whether this approach is of merit if applied to pastoral care as an activity of all Christians outside specialist counseling settings. Here the important value is the willingness to enter the reality of the other person's world at his or her pace and with methods that adequately encounter the painful and the healing features of that world. Here *story* rather than theory must become the mode both of understanding the problem and of offering care. The following incident illustrates what can happen when the world of theoretical "care" intrudes upon an individual's reconciliation through story:

> Ruth was in her fifties, unmarried, and at the top of her career. On being told she had terminal cancer she asked a friend to let her minister know. He visited her every two weeks at her home until she went into a nursing home, when he visited her weekly until her death. Most of the time the visits followed a pattern, with Ruth setting the tone of each visit. At times she wanted to talk about her illness and dying and faith, and on other occasions she would want to discuss plans for the vacation she intended to take once she was better. After the first such conversation she laughed and said, "I know of course that I will never get better, but it is fun to plan a vacation." After that the vacation became a game which both Ruth and the minister enjoyed playing.
>
> Ruth gradually became weaker and then developed acute pneumonia. As she lost consciousness she was composed and at peace. The doctors put her on a course of antibiotics and eventually managed to cure the pneumonia so that Ruth regained consciousness.
>
> When the minister next saw her she was bitter. "I did my dying and now I must do it again." She was now a changed person and visits were very difficult. She withdrew into herself, refused to be drawn into conversation, and had absolutely no interest in her vacation game.

The medical intervention in Ruth's dying broke right across the stories she was sharing with her minister, leaving her bereft of the capacity to cope in her own way with her terminal illness. Such disregard of the individual is something pastoral care should avoid by its different attitude to time. The church lives in a time between resurrection and the end of time, when all value is derived from the Lord of time and all hope depends upon the eternity of the love he has revealed. In this context there should be nothing more precious than the struggle of individuals to know and respond to their own story in their own time. Where has life led them? Where will it lead? Does it all mean hope or despair? How can we reconcile ourselves to our own story, so that we can respond with warmth and interest to the stories of others? For, in telling stories of our lives, we do not merely indulge in egocentricity. We learn to locate ourselves in others' worlds and to open our imaginations to their hopes and fears.

A campus pastor describes how one student went to great lengths to tell his story, seeking in his loneliness someone who would help him find his bearings in a world collapsing around him:

David is the youngest of three brothers who come from a broken home. All three have been intelligent and able and have entered university life. David started his studies two years ago and from the outset had shown considerable promise in his subject. However, campus life highlighted his loneliness and his need for attention. He drank heavily and rapidly faced financial difficulties. The year proved disastrous, with failure in exams and his girlfriend killed in a car accident. He left college and became involved in the drug scene. Throughout this time, when he was in the area, he visited the campus chaplaincy to talk over his difficulties. This sometimes involved a five-mile walk.

Life is still bewildering for him, although he hopes to reenter college this year. David is one of many suffering these problems. The Christian faith is frequently limited and structured so that a casualty such as David finds it alienating for him and there is no sense of freedom. Openness and sharing his difficulties was a revelation for him. His pain is well summarized by Michael Quoist: "The cry comes principally from the young, who, before they can be anesthetized and smothered by the urge to 'have' scream out their hunger to 'be'".

There is great simplicity in the pastoral care that enables others to tell their stories. Yet it also demands a discipline. Often it may appear tedious and boring to be mainly the recipient of endless reminiscences. Often people will inundate us with self-pitying tales full of unhealed wounds and recriminations. Here the discipline enters, for care does not consist merely in being a passive recipient of another's storytelling. The act of telling is itself either creative or destructive, and the hearer's involvement is crucial. A story should evoke emotion—amuse, or enlighten, or move to tears. Our participation in the story, our response (perhaps positive, perhaps honestly negative) can help the other tell the story more passionately, and by this response we help toward reconciliation or fresh understanding.

The healing power of story is already familiar to us in Christian worship and teaching. In one sense, the same story is repeated over and over again through the ages, as the church rehearses the events of the gospel. In another sense, it is a fresh story each time—created anew in the minds and hearts of the hearers through the personal involvement of those who teach and preach. This lesson from Christian education and proclamation applies to our pastoral ministry of listening. Creative and participative listening changes the dead letter of a person's tale to a living drama in which hope may be found, perhaps in an episode yet to be told.

The Passion for Truth

The final aspect of the distinctiveness of pastoral care—its passion for truth—follows naturally from its commitments to risk-taking presence and to listening to story. It has been rightly pointed out that pastoral care, like Rogerian psychotherapy, mediates acceptance of the other.[5] But this acceptance also has a special quality derived from Christian hope. Pastoral care has a future orientation which cannot remain content with the given, but seeks also the yet-to-be, the end of the story. So the physical presence and listening in pastoral care are rarely wholly passive, nondirective, or accepting in a nonconfronting sense. They express a love that seeks truth, while yet conscious of the dangers of a judgmentalism that can impede that search. Pastoral care offers an acceptance that is radical and revolutionary in its effects, because it will not tolerate half-truths or evasions. It is an acceptance face-to-face with sin, not an acceptance that sees no evil in individual or society.[6]

The problem that confronts us in this aspect of pastoral care is that of effective communication. For what are we to do when we become victims of other people's self-deceptions? How can we challenge them in a way that promotes growth? And how can the destructive features of our society's hypocrisies be countered by our seemingly insignificant protests? It is often hard to discern truth, but harder still to help it flourish in human society as we know it.

In the case that follows we see an extreme example of the Christian concern of a minister and congregation allowing themselves to become the victims of a person's untrue story. Yet when the truth emerges at least the possibility of a different kind of help is created.

Sheila is in her late twenties. She telephoned the minister to make an appointment. The story was very complicated, indicating a bad relationship with parents and a great deal of ill health.

Her full story emerged over three months: a malignant tumor on the kidney meant the removal of the kidney, and there were now secondary or tertiary tumors on the remaining kidney, the throat, the breast, the uterus, the bowel, and one that had penetrated the gall bladder. She received monthly spinal injections and attended the oncology clinic of a local hospital regularly for radiotherapy. She was in great pain and distress. Sheila demanded more and more of the minister's time, but nothing that was said or done ever seemed to help. Telephone calls and letters also came regularly. Eventually the minister approached a hospital chaplain to ask if counseling could be given when Sheila went into the hospital to have a bowel operation. The chaplain was extremely helpful but puzzled to find the name of the "surgeon," who was in fact a gynecologist. After further discussion with this chaplain, with the gynecologist, and with chaplains in two other hospitals it transpired that Sheila's story was completely untrue. There was no malignancy; there had been no radiotherapy or other medical treatment. She had a long history of treatment in the local mental hospital, which had now closed its doors to her. The minister felt anger at the time "wasted," then amusement at the memory of the misdirected prayers for healing—or were they misdirected? He and the congregation had been sucked into Sheila's desperate need to be loved. How could they help her now? The minister decided to talk honestly and directly to Sheila's parents and to Sheila herself about what he now knew. The result was a close pastoral relationship with the parents and a quite new phase in the relationship with Sheila, who began by being reproachful and anxious to please but then cut herself off entirely from the minister.

Clearly the minister who tried to help Sheila had allowed himself to be drawn into her story in an uncritical way. He had failed to notice the warning signs of an extremely demanding and infantile personality, whose seeking for attention should not have been taken as a literal statement of the truth of her condition. For Sheila, the dramatic language of cancer, with its vivid associations with contamination and death,[7] was a way of crying out for help in the midst of her chaos. Better training and better supportive supervision of those who try to pastor to such disturbed and dependent people might result in a quicker resolution of the pathological relationship and an easier transition to a help in which manipulation is fearlessly challenged. The ministry of love should be far different from unwitting collusion in self-destructive dependency, and the "fool for Christ's sake" is not the same as the "fall guy."[8]

Yet when all this has been said, the uncovering of truth can also emerge from the stumbling efforts of any person to respond to what they see in the other. Sometimes the truth emerges because we have *not* tried to be clever or cautious in our responses to others:

A theology student from Britain, serving in a church in Canada during his summer vacation, discovered Tom in a room by himself in a hospital. The student's immediate reaction on seeing Tom was to say, "My, you've got a fine suntan!" This was a very stupid thing to say because he should have realized that Tom's yellow face was not due to the sun but to severe jaundice.

Yet this most unprofessional remark proved to be the best thing he could have said. Until that moment, no one, neither hospital staff nor relatives, had dared to say anything about the yellow complexion Tom himself had seen developing in the mirror. It opened the doors to communication. Tom talked about the jaundice, of his fears of cancer, of his childhood in Britain, and of the joy of breeding greyhounds. A week later Tom was dead, having left instructions that he wished the student to conduct his funeral.

Thus the important point is not *how* the truth is reached, whether as a result of the new perceptions given by training or as a result of our naive stumbling into an area where others fear to tread. Rather, it is the willingness to find truth that alone matters. Training in itself provides no guarantee that this quest will be followed, since often the generalizations of theory merely obscure the unique truth for this person at this time. Instead there must be a passion for truth in those who care for others, a discarding of unquestioned assumptions and a willingness to share in the pain others must feel, if we are to help them overcome their illusions and self-deceptions about themselves and their futures. *Not* to promise a rose garden means to be willing to be a companion in deserts and dark places, where the dryness and the terror may oppress us also. In the ultimate questions of life, death, forgiveness, and meaning with which pastoral care must deal, there is no training that can make the helper feel secure in a knowledge gained before the encounter.

This quest for truth in pastoral care is well expressed in the following description by a prison chaplain of his struggles to care for prisoners sentenced to life imprisonment for murder:

We have to convince the prisoner and be convinced ourselves that we are men who stand in understanding of each other. We have to persuade a man that he is equal to us and we are equal to him. The attitude of the prisoner very often is that we do not stand beside him. We must use what power we have to convince him that William Blake got it right in "The Gates of Paradise" when he said,
> Mutual forgiveness of each vice,
> Such are the gates of paradise.

Until we have learned to forgive each other and to meet as man to man we cannot get closer. In professional roles the feeling often is, Me up here as the carer and you down there as the problem. We must try to know what it really is like, that at 5:00 P.M., the prisoner is shut in, you go home.

BEYOND PROFESSIONALISM

I have spoken throughout this chapter of a "structure" whereby pastoral care may find its own professionalism. But it must be evident that the structure I have offered lacks the strength and the rigidity that one might require in order to create a *secure* professionalism. There is an untidiness or open-endedness in pastoral care, as I have been describing it. It does not relate to any specific group within the church. Moreover, one cannot readily formulate a policy, specify techniques, or design an educational curriculum on the basis of such wide-reaching commitments as bodily presence, hearing stories, seeking truth. These are really just ways of being with people that can inform a wide range of actions from simple neighborly concern to the most skilled and intensive psychotherapy. In short, what I have been describing is much more a way of *being* than a way of *doing*. That is why, despite the fact that it entails a public declaration and can be enhanced by training, pastoral care also goes beyond professionalism. It cannot remain the preserve of a professional group.

The reason for this transcendence of professionalism can be found in the character of the Christian life. Because of the pervasiveness of sin, this life can never be one of secure adjustment to society. Inherent in the gospel is the voice of prophecy which fearlessly exposes injustice, corruption, and exploitation of the weak by the powerful, and which longs passionately for peace and mutual love. Even if Christians often lack the ability to speak prophetically, the manner in which they are called upon to live in their daily lives represents a fundamental challenge to every human society.

Thus the truth of pastoral care must finally be a truth that sets us free from the security of an acknowledged social status. Professionalism, by its nature, depends on society. It conserves institutions, smoothes out irregularities in social life, maintains the familiar social order, and finds a place within it for those who practice a profession. But pastoral care must be able to cast aside all such things if truth demands it, or if love points in a different way. Pastoral care finds no security *within* the city walls. It must also go out into the wilderness, if that is where the spirit of God will be found. In the next chapter we must consider how people can be prepared for this hard pilgrimage to a loving that lacks the security of an authorized role and status in caring for others.

CHAPTER 5

Preparing, Being, and Doing

Experience is a futile teacher
Experience is a prosy preacher
Experience is a fruit tree fruitless
Experience is a shoe-tree bootless
For sterile wearience and drearience
Depend, my boy, upon experience.
                    Ogden Nash, "Experience to Let"

The claim to offer an effective professional service to others is substantiated by the evidence that each practitioner has undergone a period of study and testing in order to develop the appropriate skills and gain the relevant knowledge. A pastoral care that moves beyond the security of professional status must not leave this requirement behind. It must still be consistent and trustworthy helping. It requires some form of disciplined preparation in order to be responsibly exercised. Neither "education" nor "training," however, seems quite the right term to describe the preparation required for pastoral care. A more fitting word may be "formation," even though it can carry overtones of indoctrination and of a stereotyped image of ministry. "Formation" entails not merely the acquisition of knowledge or the fostering of skills, but also the development of character. It suggests that a state of being must precede any action, any doing. It implies a holistic approach to those undergoing preparation, one that deals with their emotions, attitudes, and value commitments, so far as these relate to the knowledge and skills required for pastoral care.

In considering the nature of such formation it is worth beginning with Ogden Nash's dictum, "Experience is a futile teacher." It is a common fallacy to suppose that we can learn simply from the process of living itself. As Nash expostulates later in the poem, "Experience! Wise men do not need it! Experience! Idiots do not heed it!" We do *not* learn from experience as such. We learn only if we develop ways of reflecting upon experience. If this reflection is omitted then all that experience does is to confirm us in habitual ways of thinking and acting. "Formation" for pastoral care could mean merely the substitution of an alternative set of habits inculcated according to some common orthodoxy. But the formation we shall be exploring in this chapter is very different from such indoctrination. It entails the nurturing of creativity and sensitivity, the fostering of a "divine discontent," and the promotion of the quietness that comes from wisdom. None of these qualities can be forced upon another person, but few of us can gain them even to a small degree without help or guidance. Formation for pastoral care provides us with the means of turning our experience into lessons in humility and love by sharpening our capacity to reflect upon the past and to open ourselves to the future.

KNOWLEDGE AND CREATIVITY

The connection between knowing and doing in professional work is often thought to be a comparatively straightforward one. Those areas of human knowledge are studied that appear to have direct application to the professional tasks. Thus doctors study anatomy, physiology, pharmacology, and so on, in order to prepare themselves for the tasks of diagnosis, prognosis, and prescription of treatment. For social workers, on the other hand, subjects like psychology, sociology, and law are thought to be more appropriate. Whether the connection between knowledge and practice in these fields is really such a simple one is a question that can be left aside in this book.[1] The question of relevance and appropriateness arises in a much more acute form in the context of formation for pastoral care, because it can have no simple "knowledge base."

With the development of training in counseling methods and the "learning from living human documents" of the Clinical Pastoral Education movement, it has been assumed that the relevant body of knowledge for pastoral care will be found in a combination of traditional theological study with an exposure to the human sciences, in particular dynamic psychology, psychotherapeutic theory, and small group theory. Such a view sees "religious resources" being brought to bear on the problems of human development and interpersonal relationships, which are uncovered by such subject matters. This approach has much to commend it, especially in the psychologically disruptive surroundings of modern postindustrial Western society, but it has certain serious limitations. First, it tends to see formation for pastoral care as a finishing process within education for the full-time ministry. Thus, in effect, it excludes the preparation of the whole membership of the church. Second, it fails to consider whether theological study might not *itself* be an appropriate preparation for pastoral care. Third, it tends to freeze pastoral care in the images of human need and distress created by contemporary depth psychology, without providing the means for demythologizing the current world view, exposing its cultural and historical relativity and its inadequate imagery.

A formation for pastoral care committed to the release of the power of love among the whole community of Christians must attempt to circumvent these limitations. This is not a simple task, since *any* knowledge base that is chosen will have a limiting effect of some kind. But a guideline may be sought in the concept of creativity. Creativity consists in the use of the self's uniqueness to produce some "new thing." It can be a painful and risky process, since it takes effort to avoid the comfortable repetition of the past, and there is often a fear of failure, ridicule, or even loss of self. The parenting of a child is a familiar (though often only partially understood) example of creativity. The uniqueness of father and mother is brought together to produce a new being who is like them, yet also different. There is pain and risk in childbirth, and balanced with the joys of parenthood is the sense of responsibility that it brings and the fear of loss of freedom or of failure to cope.

Thus creativity entails having the courage to give oneself to a future whose nature is only partially glimpsed. It is commitment to the new—not to some passing fad or fashion, but to something that comes from the self and that yet has its own dynamic of development. The knowledge that undergirds pastoral care must have a demand for creativity at its center. It cannot be passively assimilated or mechanically applied. It must draw out the creativity of the learner, requiring a risking of self, imposing a cost, issuing a challenge, opening a vision. This cannot be achieved merely be adding academic subjects to a theological curriculum. It requires a transformation in method and attitude toward the task of formation in the church as a whole. Above all, it requires an overcoming of the split between intellect, emotion, and imagination so often created in traditional education.

We may speak more specifically about such creativity in knowledge by considering how we might prepare people to offer pastoral care in the following situations:

(1)

Jack is a television critic, aged forty-five, married, with two children. In his heyday he seemed a godlike man whose services to society were spectacular. His aged parents who lived with him were "tight" Methodists and they restricted his life in many ways. His wife loved him dearly and often boasted about how well she got on with Jack. In a way, she worshiped him.

Jack obtained a job that kept him in the public eye and took him into a heavy-drinking society. He gradually began to boast about his achievements and success. This was such a radical departure from his former style that his friends began to wonder what was happening to him.

His problem could be seen in terms of pride. He was lauded as an intellectual, and gradually shunned the church on the pretext that he had to monitor television output on Sundays. He became so sophisticated that the church could not hold him. When he needed help, therefore, he would go to no one at all. He gradually became seriously addicted to alcohol, and eventually his wife left for another city, where she stayed. From then on her husband's character deteriorated. He never did get proper treatment, and today, after twelve years, he is a broken man who might in other circumstances have become a great national leader.

(2)

Anne, in her late thirties, is single, lives with a widowed aunt, and has suffered from agoraphobia for nine years. She is in contact with a local group and receives visits from the leader of the group, though she refuses to go to the group herself, giving as her reason a dislike of being with people all afflicted as she is. She has been to a faith healer, and is in touch by telephone and letter with other societies (at some distance), seeking to find physical causes for her condition. She is bitter about the falling away of her friends and is careful not to "bore" anyone with her troubles.

The pastoral visitor is "entertained" by a succession of amusing anecdotes from her past, when she traveled abroad and found excitement in big cities. The impression is given of an adventurous and outgoing personality. But now Anne is constantly comparing herself with others and finding herself wanting, despite the fact that she is an extremely attractive and intelligent woman with a friendly manner.

Although able occasionally to visit relatives by car and to make brief sorties in the local streets, Anne spends most of her time in bed or indoors in dressing gown and slippers, with little company apart from her aunt and the television.

(3)

John is approaching thirty and married. He and his wife are both church members. John came to my vestry one evening and told me that his marriage had never been consummated. "I want to, but Betty thinks it's dirty." John and Betty had already, through their own doctor, been seeing a psychiatrist who had been taking them through a scheme of sexual education—attempts at sexual expression three times a week and a list of things to try to do.

John and Betty had agreed that I be approached. John presented it as Betty's problem, and I was expected to visit her while he worked late at the office.

Betty was one of three children in an excessively hard-working family. Her father broke strikes because of his drive to work. Her mother still worked in a factory. Sister and brother had "done well" and were teachers. The family home was in the suburban belt. Betty's mother had *never* talked about babies, menstruation, or sex. Betty sees herself as "the stupid member of the family." When she was eighteen she had gone to an office party, gotten slightly drunk, and advances were made by a married man. "Did you have intercourse together?" "I don't think so." She feels dirty and ashamed. She has to be in control now. No drink at all. Everything in John and Betty's flat is clean and shining. She lays out John's clean clothes for him every night as though he were her baby.

John has a problem in maintaining, and nowadays even in achieving, an erection. It is convenient to blame Betty, and she is used to blame and accepts it.

A notable feature of these three cases is that they all present problems that have a medical or psychiatric aspect—alcoholism, agoraphobia, sexual inhibition, and neurotic obsessiveness. Yet a pastoral understanding must be different in character from a medical understanding of the unhappiness that deadens the lives of Jack, Anne, John, and Betty. Obviously a knowledge of the medical aspects of these cases could be useful for someone offering pastoral care. Frequently what is required is a supportive role, where an understanding of the treatment available can be of great practical use. But an *imaginative* pastoral care will also attempt to go beyond the clinical, psychiatric, or psychotherapeutic, to human dimensions which may easily be overlooked. Creativity in pastoral care requires more than merely being a backup or ancillary service to the "real" professionals. It entails offering something new, something that may be sparked by the friction a theological understanding of human nature offers. It is from the worship, educational programs, and life style of local congregations that the distinctive creativity of pastoral care must emerge.

How might such theological creativity find expression in a care that is relevant to these people's unhappiness? It would be presumptuous to try to offer theological "solutions" to the deeply distressing problems sketched in these brief case reports. But a direction of thinking can be suggested—a direction that should be sought in all preparation for pastoral care that seeks to give it a *distinctive* helping role. In the case of Jack the notion of "pride" needs to be examined. Who helps people like Jack with their "godlikeness," which attracts worshipers only as long as the "god" is likeable? Who is with Jack when pride turns to dust and ashes, and wife and friends no longer care for him? Traditionally, theology has seen pride as a principal feature of human sinfulness, since it makes humans want to be like God and so leads them away from their true peace. The overcoming of this pride is found in the humility of Jesus, who sought no reputation, but became the despised and rejected one out of his love for the poor and the outcast. These theological themes need to find a place in the *being* of those who offer pastoral care to the casualties of human self-aggrandizement like Jack. Thus the formation required is one that takes theology out of the textbooks and into the everyday hopes and fears that influence our own choices in life. The person who knows his or her own destructive pride knows well the childish anxiety that makes Jack seek out fame and praise and the consolation of the liquor bottle. Only such a person can stay close to Jack in his alcoholic misery, can persevere as a friend through the manipulations of his alcoholic game playing without giving up hope. Only the person who has struggled through pride to unpretentious humility will have the strength of character to keep trying to create newness in the seemingly closed book of Jack's life, for true humility perseveres without needing the guarantee of success.

Thus formation for pastoral care requires imaginative applications and explorations of seemingly abstract and generalized theological ideas. It is an adventurous *personalizing* of theology, which must include the learner's own person. In the case of Anne, perhaps the theme of the alien, the stranger, needs to be explored. That is how Anne feels in every situation, except the safest and the most familiar. Beyond the safe confines of her own room she is utterly vulnerable and lost in fear. Where then to start such a theological exploration? With Jesus' cry of dereliction on the cross, perhaps? Or with the lamentations of the Jewish exiles, as they weep by the rivers of Babylon? Or with those moments in our own lives when suddenly our habitual defenses seem stripped away and we feel utterly alone, abandoned like little children in a terrifying darkness? As with pride, so with alienation, we cannot offer pastoral care out of an abstract concept. We offer it when the really frightening aspects of our daily encounters, in all the noise, speed, and demands for competence of modern life, come home to us anew. Then, and only then, can we make the imaginative leap that may help to welcome the stranger, to find the place where the lost one wanders, and perhaps to lead her gently back to human warmth. The way we are, so finely balanced between a necessary defensiveness and an innovative openness, makes us creators of new and hope-inspired relationships. The promised land, the return from exile, the kingdom within and among us, the resurrection of the body which was dead in its fearfulness and abandonment—all such hopes are empty phrases, unless they are given creative expression in the being of those who care.

John and Betty present perhaps the most unnerving and difficult problem for those seeking to offer creative pastoral help. They are so thoroughly enmeshed in their anxieties and loss of confidence that it would seem very difficult for anyone unskilled in sexual therapy or in the treatment of neurosis to be of much help. Moreover, as we noticed in the previous chapter, the bodily and the sexual are areas in which the Christian tradition has had little positive to offer, so great has been the fear of passion and carnality. Yet John and Betty seem unable to gain much from psychiatric help, and they turn to the church for some kind of understanding or relief of unhappiness. Here the creativity called for is one that fearlessly explores the nature of *embodied* love.

The central Christian doctrine of incarnation is one that can seem shocking in its implications for those who want a wholly spiritualized faith. It locates the love of God unambiguously within the body[2] and finds its invincibility in the simplest of bodily expressions. In Christ love is incarnate from the helplessness of the infant to mature manhood. Love is found in the womb of

Mary and at her breast. Love dwells in the growing boy and in the mature man, whose ministry brings him a woman's tears for water and her hair for a towel, whose burial is prepared for by precious ointment poured upon the head, whose risen body Mary Magdalene seeks to embrace. The tender language of the body is not spurned by the Word of God incarnate. We may fear the body's ambiguity and its nonrational dynamic, but the goodness of enfleshed love is given eternal significance by the purity of Christ's passion. So creative pastoral ministry with John and Betty will not be trapped by their fears and anxieties, but will radiate the warmth of a love that casts out fear.

Once again formation for pastoral care must mean the *personalizing* of theological ideas: incarnate love becomes a reality in the release from anxiety about our sexuality and a joyful acceptance of our bodily selves. This does not, of course, mean a magic resolution of Betty's obsessiveness and John's impotence. They have a long and painful struggle ahead if such deep-seated problems are to be overcome. (In sexual relationships the element of spontaneity is so central that, once it has been lost, deliberate efforts to recover it may prove counterproductive.) But what they can receive, from those who would help them in the power of the gospel of love, is the comfort of nonthreatening tenderness and the encouragement of people whose bodies are felt to be sources of joy, not shame. Thus formation for pastoral care must include a theological awareness that finds honest, unembarrassed, and pure expression in bodily terms. Such adventurous creativity is rarely found in traditional theological education, which rests content with an explanation that satisfies and stimulates the mind alone. But the knowledge base for pastoral care cannot be merely intellectual in character if it is to produce genuine care.

FRAGILITY, SENSITIVITY, AND SKILL

Closely allied to the tension between creativity and knowledge which we have just discussed, there is a second tension—between sensitivity and skill. If preparation for pastoral care is regarded as "education," then it may concentrate solely on intellectual development; if it is regarded as "training," then the concentration tends to be on techniques, effective behavior patterns, skills. But formation for pastoral care needs to avoid both of these extremes. In the place of intellectualism and of pragmatism, it seeks to develop an attitude that combines self-criticism and competence in a creative tension. This aspect of formation can be best described by focusing on *fragility* in human relationships.

> Beth, unmarried and in her forties, had lost her younger brother after a long illness. They had been very close and it took her some time to recover. The rest of her family supported her well in her bereavement. Two years later she lost her mother, a difficult old lady, whom she had faithfully cared for and then visited regularly in an old people's home. To her bewilderment, she found that she could feel nothing about her mother's death, but instead began to grieve for her brother all over again. The experience upset her greatly.
> She untied the tangle with a minimum of help. She realized that she was very angry with her mother for years of slights and deliberately difficult behavior. The old lady's death was a relief, not a burden. At the same time, part of Beth felt that grief was the appropriate response to bereavement, and so produced grief again for someone whose death had been a real loss.

There is nothing very unusual in Beth's reaction to loss, and she was able to deal with her experience constructively with just a minimum of help, but her situation is a parable of the human condition which we easily forget. We carry loss as a constant companion by virtue of our humanity. Indeed, we might describe loss as the most typical and pervasive of all human experiences.[3] We are mortals who depend upon, cherish, and mourn our fellow mortals. This is the essential fragility of our personal world. We spin the delicate fibers of love, making connections that must inevitably be brushed aside by death. Such fragility is by no means denied by doctrines of resurrection or of eternal life, since the whole force of such doctrines is that death is no illusion, but a reality that can only be countered by life of a different kind from the one that we know and treasure.

The quality of care offered to another is dependent upon the delicate handling of this fragility. The sensitivity required is not easily gained, since it is not to be confused with well-meaning but undiscriminating sympathy or with highly sophisticated counseling techniques. On occasion, simple sympathy or skilled counseling may indeed be required, but the more basic and widespread requirement is for helpers who are not afraid to acknowledge the painful insecurity that surrounds us all, and that enters all aspects of our lives. This is to live without denying death, and few of us find such realism easy to maintain. As a result, the unresolved grief in other people's lives can often leave us feeling powerless to help:

> Mr. and Mrs. Jones had an only son. He was killed while on active duty in Cyprus. His room is now a memorial to him. Life stopped for his parents at his death. Their relationships with other people are determined by the intensity of the friends' observance of the son's life and death. Few friends last the course, and Mr. and Mrs. Jones move from one intense friendship to another, unable to discover any foundation to life. The minister visits regularly but is bewildered by the situation, and is unable to enter into the lasting "memorial" talk they enjoy.

No one can finally avoid the fragility of human life, and one sees much pain ahead for Mr. or Mrs. Jones when one of them is left alone by yet another death. The skill and sensitivity required in pastoral care stem from the stark realism of the Christian gospel. At its heart is a narrative of the horrifying death of a young man, who was deeply loved and deeply mourned, and who died unjustly. In the sacrament of Communion that death is constantly memorialized, as a sign not of enduring grief, but of perfect hope. Those who celebrate that death, who rejoice in its defeat through the resurrection and who look forward to the final victory that is promised, have an attitude to life that both honors sorrow and transcends it. The skill of pastoral care—if skill is the right word—consists in reaching out to the many griefs that people cannot face and offering the healing of a fearless vulnerability. This is certainly not to imply that any one person can avoid all evasions and denials or can remain sensitive to every nuance of unresolved sorrow in others. Rather, out of the fellowship of those "who show the Lord's death till he come," there can emerge the qualities required for a pastoral care that skillfully tends wounds until they heal. But that same fellowship must also tend the helpers, when the fragility of *their* most treasured relationships becomes too much for them.

The practical conclusion to be drawn from our discussion of formation for pastoral care up to this point is that the best preparation for helping others is a style of Christian living that promotes creativity and sensitivity. This, above all, is why overly stressing the training of pastoral counselors can lead the churches in precisely the wrong direction. The center of concern must be the quality of the *koinōnia* in its worship, its social life, and its personal relationships. The local church can easily evade the responsibility for the uncaring and health-destructive aspects of its week-by-week existence by singling out a group of people who are to be the experts in care and who must carry all the responsibility for the weak and the vulnerable, inside and outside the church. It is this seduction that the new generation of well-trained counseling ministers must be at pains to avoid at all costs. It is true, of course, that people with an understanding of the dynamics of counseling and with a natural aptitude or acquired skill in counseling have a leadership role to play in the Christian community. But that leadership consists in *abandoning* all claims to authority, refusing to be put in the position of the one upon whom all others can depend, casting aside the garments of status and offering oneself only in a menial task, like the lowliest servant. For not until the *koinōnia* as a whole feels its need to learn to love and seeks to live in love can the authorized, accredited helper have any place within it.

Thus formation for creativity and sensitivity must begin with the constant reformation of the church's own life. It means developing a way of worshiping together that opens the mind and the heart to the needy, developing small group meetings that are personal and supportive in a way that allows people to learn about physical and emotional closeness, offering educational opportunities where experts, not only in psychology but also in theology, can help church members explore the religious dimensions of the daily demands of loving others. In the context of a church actively seeking to learn and grow in ordinary caring, the trained counselor can offer special skills in guidance, supervision, and contact with professional helping agencies. But if that context is missing, then such counselors are merely slaves to the conscience of a church too preoccupied with its own survival to see the neighbor's need as its responsibility. Unless the local congregation is a warm, supportive, open, and honest fellowship, it denies all opportunity for a true ministry of pastoral care.

A DIVINE DISCONTENT

Yet formation for pastoral care will still fail if it is concerned only with developing theological creativeness and skilled sensitivity in a warm fellowship. The hardest part of formation is that which constantly brings back the sharp reminder of the kerygma, the preaching of the challenge of the gospel of love. Such preaching is not only about love in personal encounters, when one individual may attempt a sensitive care for another. The kerygma is about a love that encompasses all humankind and all human history with a power that both judges and affirms. This prophetic edge of the gospel cuts across the too easy translation of pastoral care into care for individuals only. Instead it creates a "divine discontent," demanding that humanity gain a vision of itself that shows its defacing of the divine image. Thus repentance, reappraisal, and a turning again to pursue good and fight evil, must all characterize the attitude of those who claim a pastoral concern for others.

This aspect of formation for pastoral care has often been bypassed by the popular "clinical model" in training for pastoral care and counseling. The useful methods of verbatim analysis and individual and group supervision developed in this context do not transfer effectively to the sociopolitical arena. Perhaps the most obvious problem is that the qualities required for the effective, empathetic counselor are quite different from those required for effective political influence. The prophet cannot have the comfort of being found to be warm, flexible, and non-judgmental by the powers that prophecy must challenge. Rather, prophecy cuts cross-grained to society, exposing at its cutting edge the hidden layers of influence and power. Such prophetic confrontation should not be confused with confrontational techniques in counseling or psychotherapy, for within the therapeutic context the challenge is only to individual responsibility. But in the divine discontent of prophetic pastoral care the target is the social fabric itself, with its interwoven patterns of unjust influence and power. Outside the safe confines of the counseling setting the risks are much greater. Those who proclaim love in the face of industrial, political, and military power raise up the forces that crucified Christ and that continue to react with violence to any serious challenge to their dominance in society. As Peter Selby reminds us:

> A spiritual or psychological practice that does not seek to locate its participants in relation to the perpetrators of oppression in the world outside and to its victims has no contribution to make to the realization of human potential, let alone to the encounter of the person with the God whose commitment is to the struggle for justice, freedom and peace.[4]

Thus formation for pastoral care must devise new methods for identifying and implementing the prophetic message of love of neighbor—of *every* neighbor without partiality. The gospel must be preached in word and action. This entails thorough biblical and theological study by those who preach and a full critical exposure to the political and liberation theologies that have emerged in countries where social injustice is at its most extreme. The challenge of such theologies must be felt, whatever criticisms may also be leveled against them, since they represent a thorough attempt to recover the communal aspects of Christianity, so muted in our era by individualist assumptions about religious faith. At the same time, such formation should not remain at the level of exhortation and critical scrutiny in intellectual terms. The challenge is not simply to thought but to action, and from the discontent with violence, injustice, and social discrimination in society there should emerge concrete proposals for action.

Thus formation of the church's membership should include project work in which specific proposals are formulated for meeting social needs, and the implementation of these proposals attempted and then critically evaluated. Only by such quite specific efforts at involvement is it possible to help people acquire an insight into the *politics* of love and to understand why so often idealism in political life is destroyed by apathy or by a sense of futility. There are few situations as yet where Christians who profess to love are given the opportunity of experiencing the moral ambiguity of political life or of discovering through personal experience the strength of opposition to any change that undermines political power. Formation for pastoral care needs to include some exposure to the discomfort, danger, and humiliation of following in the footsteps of Jesus.

(1)

Iris is a middle-aged woman who suffers from severe disabilities. She cannot walk without braces and can only barely cope with simple household tasks. She has never married, and at the time of my first contact lived alone in a house that was severely affected by damp and was in a poor state of repair. She rented her accommodation from a leading citizen who persistently refused to bring the property up to standard. Should the congregation or the minister be concerned? What might they do?

(2)

A "problem family" with a history of violence and petty theft were evicted by the authorities from their state-rented home under cover of darkness, their belongings dumped in the front garden and the door barricaded. I was able to find them overnight accommodation in a hotel annex, but when this was featured in a story in the local press the company who owned the hotel ordered the manager not to give them shelter. I then was able to obtain the loan of a house trailer, and a local businessman allowed it to be parked in his firm's storage yard. This came to an end when the family, in an effort to keep warm, started lighting open fires outside the trailer. The police visited, noted that there was an oil tank in the yard next door, and ordered the trailer to be removed. A long succession of additional problems ensued, and the family ended up by being separated and broken up.

When the father of the family died, one of the sons was allowed out of prison to attend the graveside service, chained to a detective. As soon as the service ended the other members of the family rushed to attack this detective, determined to repay at least one debt! For them all authority was alien and destructive, but they did maintain a modicum of respect for, and trust in, the church.

These two case descriptions do not lend themselves to an individualistic approach. They reveal an unfilled gap in pastoral education for minister and church members alike. How, in *concrete* terms, is the church—a community of socially respectable, relatively successful people—to fulfill its ministry to the poor, the outcast, the "failures" in society? How is love for neighbor to find effective and humble expression in a place that is a genuine home for the poor of the earth? So far little has been thought of beyond charitable institutions which offer help but remain safely exempt from the real pressures and hazards of life on the margins of society. Yet there can be no ministry of love that holds on to its own security and comfort. The truly unsettling aspects of this dimension of formation for pastoral care are as yet only to be guessed at, but they will be found when pastoral care rediscovers its communal identity and its ethical challenge to all human institutions.

There is undoubtedly an unresolved tension in this aspect of pastoral care. The search for *inner* peace in a strife-torn world is one that has always been a dominant theme in pastoral care. It is natural to look more energetically for the inner peace of the gospel than to keep returning to its painful social challenge. Because we so long for wholeness and for inner security, we are often tempted to settle for less than the whole truth, closing our eyes to the evident injustices in the world, pretending that we have no part in them, or that there is nothing we can do about them. We seek a quiet oasis in the desert of human lovelessness, and we may use our capacity to love and to care merely to encourage others to join us in this dreamlike refuge. Yet the poor continue to die, the weak to be exploited, and the rich and powerful to gain strength from our apathy. The tension is made still more uncomfortable by the obvious ambiguities in all political causes. Often it must seem that there can never be a political movement that is exempt from the corruption of self-interest or from the abuse of power. There seems to be an unavoidable compromise of principle entailed in effective political action, something less pure, less honest than the disinterested love of persons so evident in personal helping relationships.

It would seem that all formation for pastoral care must prepare people for these hard truths about our political and social life. The Christian message contains a major challenge to all naive optimism about the way in which love can find root in human life. Nothing can take away from the tragedy at the heart of the Christian gospel, that an innocent and wholly loving man was crucified by the authorities of his day. His followers dare not hope for an easier way to give love a living and active place in human history. As Peter Selby observes, we must not be childishly confident in the triumph of love. We cannot dodge the incompleteness, vulnerability, and ambiguous future of all attempts to make this world a more loving place:

> In order to be involved . . . we have to recognize that adult responsibility for the situation of humanity in history demands that we join God in the likelihood of God's defeat at the hands of a godless world.[5]

Such adult realism is a major requirement in all formation for pastoral care.

THE WISDOM OF GOD

It would be an error, however, to end this discussion of formation for pastoral care on too despairing a note. We have seen throughout this book how much ambiguity surrounds the term "professionalism" and how uncertain is its application to the field of pastoral care. I have been presenting an account of pastoral care that is sympathetic to Lambourne's description of it as "lay, voluntary and diffuse in the community."[6] My stress on the pastoral ministry of *all* Christians has meant that the formation required cannot be based on the professional training school model, but rather on the creation of an ethos within the Christian community as a whole. Yet, at the same time, the concept of professionalism as a public declaration of intent to offer service has been seen to be a useful description of a pastoral care that is more than a vague, erratic (and perhaps sentimental) commitment to be loving to others. This element of commitment and consistency is what transforms pastoral care from amateur good will to disciplined acts of care and concern.

It is in the light of this account of the "professionalism" of pastoral care that we must resist an overemphasis on success and competence. It is from a state of *being* that the *doing* must come, for here lies the consistency and commitment. The state of being from which love flows is one of quietness, and of a wisdom that sees one's own limits and inadequacies. There is always a danger that in stressing the need for imaginativeness, sensitivity, and ethical concern in pastoral care the Christian will be portrayed as some kind of heroic figure, a superior being with capacities far beyond "ordinary" humanity outside the church. Nothing could be further from the truth. Christian wisdom does not stem from an awareness of superior knowledge, or from a confidence in the purity of one's motives, but from the very opposite. The *koinōnia* is a community of self-confessed sinners whose vision of God's love serves to underline their failures. Their wisdom consists in knowing their folly, and their strength in knowing their weakness.

Thus the consistency in pastoral care will eventually be founded upon the way of repentance that characterizes the Christian life. As soon as the self-confidence of the political activist or of the personal counselor removes the need for "turning again," the professionalism of pastoral care is lost. There is a quiet center to pastoral care which consists of the person at peace once more in the wisdom of God, whose love never fails. When contact with that center is lost, Christians have nothing special to offer to their fellow humans. But when, in trying to love their neighbors, they are once more conscious of the greatness of God's love, then there is a deep tranquility that they can offer to others:

> If a man choose to enter the kingdom of peace
> he shall not cease from struggle until he fail,
> and having failed he will be astonished,
> and having been astonished will rule,
> and having ruled will rest.[7]

CHAPTER 6

The Many Faces
of Love

It is the fulfilment and the triumph of love that it is able to reunite
the most radically separated beings, namely individual persons.

Paul Tillich,
Love, Power and Justice

We may now draw together the various strands in our discussion of the relationship between pastoral care and professionalism. We have seen how the call to love God and neighbor
requires a rich account of Christian love, one that holds together
desire, attraction, friendship, and impartial, self-giving love. Professionalism may not fully respond to such a call, because it is
complex and highly ambiguous, with elements of self-interest and
power seeking intermingled with elements of social usefulness
and service of the needy. In pastoral care this ambiguity is evident
in the dominant place of the ordained clergy within a community,
all of whose members have a call to humble service. By exploring
the concept of vocation, I have argued that there need be no
essential relationship between the ordained ministry and the
church's task of pastoral care, even though on many occasions
such care can and should be offered by clergy in their representative function. The breaking of the link between clerical role and
pastoral task has led me to a reappraisal of professionalism in
pastoral care. After identifying and rejecting the "captivity" of
pastoral care by the wrong kind of professionalism, I have offered
in its place a new, looser framework derived from the community,

witness, and service of the church's life as the body of Christ. Finally, I have offered ideas for a style of preparation for pastoral care that could lead to a way of *being*, one that fosters a richer way of *doing*, in uniting love of God and love of neighbor.

It remains to consider the unity of these diverse elements in the ministry of pastoral care by returning to the richness of love. "Love" is used in so many senses that it could be misleading to assert its centrality in pastoral care. Nevertheless, if we maintain Paul Tillich's emphasis on the reunion of the separated, seen at its most powerful in the reunion of individual persons, then we can hold on to the richness. For persons are themselves complex wholes of rational and nonrational elements, all of which may participate in love of another. The love that God gives us for our well-being and flourishing is one that enters all parts of our relationships and redeems and renews them all. Pastoral care is an (often unsuccessful) striving to mediate this love to all who are alienated and lost in their sorrows. Love, so the title of this chapter suggests, has many faces, and a true pastoral care will never become restricted to one expression of love's power, but will be open and changing according to the need and the situation.

Of many possible expressions of love, we may select three as of especial importance for the reunion of separated individuals: love in order, love in presence, and love in responsibility. These three unite in the whole person, who, in intellect, emotion, and will, may try to love another.

LOVE IN ORDER

It may at times have seemed, during some of the critical analyses in earlier chapters, that the view of pastoral care expressed in this book removes all significance from the traditional ministry of pastoral care exercised by ordained clergy. This, however, is not my intention. Love can be consistently mediated only when there is some kind of order that ensures continuity and answerability. It is not a question of whether there should be order in the ministry of pastoral care, but rather of what form that order should take in order to be a true response to the call to love. The danger in the order represented only by ordination to a full-time ministry is that it may obscure the challenges and the opportunities of a caring that is more broadly based, imaginative, and informal in character. Nevertheless, it is obvious that, both in terms of opportunities for caring and in terms of means of mediating love, the ordained clergy have a significant part to play in pastoral care. This is true not only in respect of the ordained minister's pastoral relationship to members of the congregation, but also of his or her representative and symbolic role with people who have lost contact with institutional religion:

> Mrs. Brown was acutely depressed eighteen months after the tragic and sudden death of her twenty-year-old daughter in a traffic accident. The case was referred by the consultant psychiatrist to a social worker, who in turn sought the help of the hospital chaplain because Mrs. Brown, previously a regular church attender, claimed that she had "lost her faith" and been unable to return to her church since the accident. This she regretted very much, and so she gladly agreed to meet with the chaplain. Over the course of a few interviews it emerged that Mrs. Brown had not been able to face attending her daughter's funeral, but now visited the cemetery by herself each day. In order to help Mrs. Brown "say goodbye" to her daughter it was arranged (with the approval of the consultant) that one day the chaplain and the social worker would go with Mrs. Brown to the cemetery. There the chaplain conducted a short service using readings and prayers from the funeral service. Mrs. Brown experienced a slight improvement after this but it was not maintained. Eventually she was admitted to a psychiatric hospital where she received shock therapy. This appeared to be effective.

The chaplain's efforts to help Mrs. Brown were an expression of an ordered love, love mediated through the symbolism of a funeral rite. On innumerable occasions the recognized status of the ordained minister can be used in this way. The ritualization of major life events (birth, adolescence, marriage, bereavement, and death) through the ordered services of the churches, mediates a love that both supports and inspires. Moreover, when the ritual has been conducted with sensitivity and conviction, this can be an encouragement to people to seek more personal help from the minister. Occasions of formal ritual are also pastoral opportunities.

On the other hand, the order represented by ordination to the ministry of Word and Sacrament is only one example from a wide range of possibilities. Other examples could be the revitalization of the ancient order of deacon, the setting apart of a group of individuals to concentrate on the caring task; the creation of pastoral groups within congregations, with designated tasks and appropriate training; and the selection and training of specialist pastoral counselors, a major part of whose responsibility would be training and support of a wider group of helpers. These are all possible orders. None should be regarded as normative. Rather, the point must be emphasized that love without foresight, planning, and reasoned policies quickly degenerates into an erratic and partial sentimentality. Estrangement between persons is not overcome by a love that is emotion alone, but by a consistency that is fired by emotion and sustained by a critical and judicious rationality.

In the Reformed tradition the ordained minister is often described as a "teaching elder." This is a valuable emphasis, reminding us of the responsibility for preserving, interpreting, and handing on the gospel, entrusted to an educated and scholarly group within the church. The intellectual skill of the teacher, however, is only one aspect of the rationality required in caring. Equally, if not more, important is the critical balance between detachment and involvement that forms the essence of a nonexploitative helping relationship. This aspect of ordered rationality must be developed in a different, more personally confronting form of education than that offered to most ordinands (see chap. 5). The confusion between order and ordination, created by the dominant role of the prophetic and priestly ministries in the church's history, will be overcome only when the *different* gifts and *different* disciplines of the ministry of pastoral care are properly recognized. Love expressed in order requires something more adventurous than a demand for yet another competence from ministers and priests. It requires a rationality throughout the church's life, which will create new orders within and between individuals, not merely rationalize the continuity of structures inherited from the past.

LOVE IN PRESENCE

Although our rationality provides the forms within which love can be exercised, reason alone can never offer love to another person. The character of love is fundamentally nonrational or suprarational. It is an offer of self to the other person in ways that resist the cold conceptualization of language. This is very evident in the biblical narratives of the ministry of Jesus. The love Jesus offers to the poor, the outcast, and the disabled is tangible in quality. There is a reaching out, a touching, a being there, a fearless and restorative presence. The same is true of Jesus' closeness to his disciples, a closeness expressed in the fellowship of eating together, of eye contact and warm embrace, of anointing and foot washing, of tears, and of words of anger and despair. Love is presence, or it is nothing but empty form. The divide between people is overcome not by grandiloquent expressions of concern but by the simple offering of time and attention at moments of the other's need. Thus all planning and foresight in love is utterly useless if it fails to take us in a personal way to places where the need is greatest and where we are the right people to be instruments of healing and restorative love.

The difficulties in achieving such presence should not be underestimated. Often we fail to reach the other person and are left conscious of barriers we cannot break down. Often presence is a fleeting thing, felt for a moment and then lost in the flow of more anxious, more guarded thoughts and feelings. The more we strive to come close to others in their pain, the more we realize that love is a gift that cannot be summoned at will. Try as we may, our ineptitude or the anxiety of the other keeps the conversation at the level where the separation of individual selves can never be overcome.

In the following case a hospital chaplain describes how he encountered two patients in the same hospital ward who were both suffering the effects of bereavement and whose hurt feelings were brought to the surface by an invitation to attend a short service in the ward:

> I found Hilda sitting on her bed crying very sorely. The other patients were asking if I would speak to her. She told me briefly that her daughter and grandchildren had been killed in a traffic accident six months before. Her faith had been shattered. After a brief conversation she said she wanted to come to the service, and she stopped crying and came. Another patient, Betty, had joined some others from her part of the ward and had also come to the service. In the middle of the first prayer she said in a loud voice, "I'm sorry I can't take it; I'll have to leave." She got up, declined an offer to escort her back to her bed, and left. When I visited her briefly afterward she told me that a recent bereavement had led to the outburst in the service. I asked her if she would be willing to speak to me if I came back to see her the following day, and she said she would. I had also arranged to see Hilda then.
>
> When I returned the next day Hilda and Betty almost immediately began to speak of their experiences. Betty spoke of nursing three close relatives who died untimely deaths. She expressed powerful feelings of embitterment and said that she saw no point in living. She felt very much alone and said that if she were to die tomorrow, nobody would care, but she wouldn't worry in the least. As far as she was concerned, there was no God and no life after death.
>
> Hilda said she had also felt very bitter at first. The death of her daughter and her family had almost driven her mad. She got very angry with God and would have lost her faith unless her husband had helped her to see that there was no point in blaming God.

We see in this meeting with two grieving women the possibility of a personal encounter that could bring healing. They have gone through such similar feelings that each might become a minister to the other. In particular, perhaps Hilda, with her more positive resolution of anger and bitterness, could help Betty in her isolation and helplessness. Realizing these possibilities, the chaplain saw his role as that of encouraging a closer relationship between them:

> It appeared to me that the possibility of Hilda addressing Betty's pain and grief should be the basis of our discussion. At various points I tried to ask Hilda to say how she felt and to discuss Betty's bitterness with her. Although Hilda attempted to do this, she seemed unable to go beyond a restatement of her own position, in a way that failed to reach out to Betty. Eventually Betty said that she could not talk about it any more, because it was making her too upset. I tried suggesting gently that it might help her to cry out her feelings. But she said that nothing could help her and that she could not cry. There the conversation ended.

No doubt we could speculate about ways in which the chaplain might have helped Betty overcome her panic about being emotionally upset. Clearly some skill was required, which Hilda, for all her well-meaning concern, did not possess. A successful mediation by the chaplain of the acceptability and healing potential of grief and anger would have opened the way for a deeper sharing between Hilda and Betty. But the "stuckness' of the situation is perhaps closer to human reality. The counseling ideal of emotional catharsis, reparation, and recovery is not as easily achieved as we might suppose, however skilled our helping. The deep loneliness and bitterness felt by Betty is more than a symptom of unresolved grief, though clearly it is that in part. It also reflects what Tillich called "existential anxiety," a sense of the meaninglessness and futility of human life in the face of finitude and loss. Thus, while counseling skill may help, there is also a demand deeper than that of adequate technique that confronts those who offer pastoral care. Can we bring a presence to despairing people that communicates the being of a loving and utterly trustworthy God? Can we be, in the words of St. Francis, instruments of God's peace?

This, then, is love's demand—not merely to be skilled in discerning and reflecting the feelings of others, but to be present to them in such an open and peaceful way that our love and God's love seem one and the same. Hilda and the hospital chaplain knew in their heads that this was what Betty needed in order to transcend her despair. But the way of mediating such a presence eluded them both on that occasion. Who could blame them for such a failure? For, although love is one, we are all fragmented beings and it is only in rare moments that the gift comes to us to be those through whom God's presence is embodied in human love. Only rarely do mind and heart and will act as one in the harmony of love.

LOVE IN RESPONSIBILITY

Finally, in considering the oneness of love, we return to a character we met in the first chapter—Di, the colorful, banner-carrying enthusiast for political causes. For the presence of one person with another, however close, however restorative, is the beginning, not the end, of love's endeavor. From that closeness there comes a new will. When hearts of stone become once more hearts of flesh they feel again the hurts of others, escaping from the deadness of self-absorption. Thus the third expression of love is love in responsibility, an answering love that must move on if it is to be true to the goodness it has received.

Yet Di has a great personal struggle as she seeks love in responsibility. In answering the call to care for peace and justice in society she finds herself at odds with her husband and her children. She seeks to love according to her vision of goodness, but that seeking seems to deny those parts of herself that need the closeness and comfort of home and family. Indeed, when she tries to be ruthlessly honest with herself she begins to suspect that it is *precisely* her unhappiness at home that drives her into political activity. Perhaps then her love is not genuine, not truly disinterested, but merely a subtle form of self-seeking escapism.

Di's dilemma takes us to the heart of agape, the Christian love that unsettles and overturns all other loves. Jesus' preaching of the present and yet-to-come kingdom of God makes radical demands on all those who choose to follow him. Love of possessions, the security of a home, family ties and obligations—all of these take second place to the call to take up one's cross and follow him on the path of self-sacrificial love. It is a narrow gate and few can enter it, yet, paradoxically, only those who are willing to give up everything can truly find themselves. Love is letting go in order to gain all things in their true beauty. For although Jesus seems to deny family and possessions, he does so only to hallow them more deeply. He takes the ties of personal love, the family meal, the need for food, shelter, clothing, and comfort, and makes them the birthright of every needy person, however humble, however outcast, however overlooked by those whose self-satisfaction blinds them to the needs of others. So the love that is answerable to Jesus is not a cold, self-punitive, anxious striving to do good. On the contrary, it is a celebration of the goodness of human happiness, which seeks to share joy as widely as possible, breaking down the barriers between people that pride, greed, and prejudice relentlessly create.

Thus Di is on the right road, but her anxiety and unresolved conflict of loyalty reveal unhealed places in herself that may impoverish all aspects of her love for others. She needs to be helped to reunite the separated parts of her personality in order to love responsibly, in the sense of offering an *answering* love, rather than a *demanding* love. So long as she uses political activism to vent her private unhappiness she will starve both herself and those she claims to care for of all lasting goodness. Such will be her need for conflict that a peaceful resolution will be unthinkable, for it will return her to her inner emptiness. She needs to learn that love is one, that, if eros without agape is self-indulgent, then equally agape without eros is coldly impersonal. In *The Mind and Heart of Love*, Martin D'Arcy expresses well the harmony that we see lacking in Di's activism:

> There is a desire of the self to give its all and a desire to be oneself and be perfect. The principle of give and take has to be harmonized in all phases of love.[1]

The need to retain this subtle balance in responsible Christian love leads us to the general point that there can be no adequate understanding of pastoral care if moral issues are ignored. Love in responsibility is love seeking not just order and presence but righteousness. It is love so closely bound up with justice that the one cannot exist without the other. It is love that judges both the self in its poverty and ambiguity of motive, and others in their collusion in selfish disregard for human value.

What, then, is the nature of this responsible love, which integrates the person and reconciles the deep divisions between individuals and groups? We need to find a "face" that is both warm and resolute, that is steadfast but not self-righteous and narrowly judgmental. Emotion is important, yet emotion is not enough, since morality also requires consistency and self-control. It would seem that the closest one can come to an adequate description of this expression of love is to characterize it as "loyalty" or "faithfulness." H. Richard Niebuhr has a telling description of how this form of loving determines the quality of our relationships with others:

> Love is loyalty; it is the willingness to let the self be destroyed rather than that the other cease to be; it is the commitment of the self by self-binding will to make the other great.[2]

It is evident that such commitment is far removed from the minimalist arrangements for justice that exist in society as we know it. Thus Christian ethics is revolutionary, not in the simple sense that it seeks to overthrow governments, but in a more gradually corrosive sense that it refuses to accept the expediencies according to which governments gain and maintain power. Instead of regarding justice as the compromise of competing self-interests, justice-as-loyalty requires great sacrifice of self-interest in order to "make the other great," and even the sacrifice of life itself if others' lives are endangered. It is little wonder that this aspect of Christian love fails to commend itself to those who want a peaceful accommodation between church and society. It is easier to ignore the casualties of social systems than to undertake the painful task of constant confrontation with social and political power. It is easier to side with the Sanhedrin than to identify oneself as a follower of the accused Galilean.

Yet, for all its difficulties, it would seem that love in responsibility, a loyal love that seeks justice for the poorest, humblest, and least socially useful child of God, is, above all other faces, the face of love that Christ requires. We may honor God in our ordered religion, but deny him the sacrifice he truly requires (Mic. 6:6–8); we may claim devotion to the presence of love, but, in neglecting our neighbor, lose all sight of God (Matt. 25:31–46; 1 John 4:19–21). Perhaps, then, the final paradox of Christian pastoral care is that it creates a deep uneasiness with the institutions and the established routines of organized religion. Although it finds its source and inspiration in the life and worship of the gathered Christian community, the love this inspires is a new wine splitting open the old wineskins. As soon as the unity-in-diversity of Christian love is found, the person seeking to be true to *every* neighbor without partiality will almost inevitably find religious institutions constricting and insufficiently supportive of so hard and revolutionary a task. That which should nurture love can so clearly kill it, as William Blake bitterly suggests in his anticlerical poem, "The Garden of Love":

I went to the Garden of Love,
And saw what I never had seen:
A Chapel was built in the midst,
Where I used to play on the green.

And the gates of this Chapel were shut,
And "Thou shalt not" writ over the door;
So I turn'd to the Garden of Love
That so many sweet flowers bore;

And I saw it was filled with graves,
And tomb-stones where flowers should be;
And priests in black gowns were walking their rounds,
And binding with briars my joys & desires.[5]

Yet this need not be, if love remains one; and if in physical joy, in the freshness of friendship, and in the inspiration of beauty there is allowed to blossom that neighbor-love for which the Christ, worshiped by the "priests in black gowns," laid down his life. Love has many faces, but it also has one: the face of Christ, confronting our failures in love, but never failing to forgive us and so restore in us the unity of love.

LOVE'S FUTURE

It remains to suggest a few practical implications that may be drawn from the view of professionalism in pastoral care put forward in this book. These may be quite briefly summarized, since they have already emerged at various points in the course of the argument. They must be regarded as tentative and provisional in character. The specific requirements for the ministry of pastoral care vary widely from situation to situation and are altered by historical circumstances. Nevertheless, I would suggest that it is in this general direction that the future of pastoral care as a ministry of love is to be found.

Professionalism and the Clergy

The need to encourage a diversity of gifts within the Christian community requires great caution in allocating a dominant role to ordained ministers in the task of pastoral care. Instead, leadership in *koinōnia* and *diakonia* should be sought from the whole membership. Rather than seeking a specialist counseling role, clergy should specialize in the pastoral aspects of their preaching and priestly functions and should use their position of leadership in the congregation to encourage the caring ministry of all Christians. The monopolistic tendencies inherent in a collegial group like the ordained clergy must be countered by a renewed emphasis on ministry as humble service. When counseling expertise is acquired, it is not a status to be guarded but a gift to be freely shared.

Professionalism and Formation

Professionalism, in the sense of special knowledge, skill, and dedication, is certainly required in pastoral care. These attributes should be fostered in general schemes of adult Christian education, which combine insights from counseling and psychotherapy with theological reflection on human need. Theological education (education for full-time ministry) should concentrate on providing an appropriately trained teaching ministry for this task of formation within the local congregation. Such formation should integrate worship, study, and experience in supportive groups and practical involvement. Formation must take place within the context of a *koinōnia* that is open to the world.

Professionalism and Reformation

Finally, conservative tendencies in professionalism must be countered by the radical critique of all institutions that comes from love as agape. The motto *ecclesia reformata semper reformanda est* (a reformed church always requires to be reformed) applies as much to the pastoral ministry of churches as to other aspects of their life, and it need not be applied only to churches claiming the designation "Reformed." On the contrary, it is in encounter between different church traditions and in open dialogue between Christian churches and other religious and secular groups concerned with human welfare that flexibility in institutional form may be learned. A feature of the "professionalism" that Christians espouse is the awareness that without God's grace nothing can be achieved. This feature results in a refusal to make idols out of churches or other organizations. Pastoral care must always be iconoclastic, especially of its own most treasured images. It will seek love where it is to be found, remembering that God's incarnate love knows none of the boundaries that human complacency creates, but that the body of Christ is alive in the most unexpected places, where humble service meets human need.

Notes

CHAPTER 1

1. Reinhold Niebuhr, *An Interpretation of Christian Ethics* (1935; reprint, New York: Meridian Books, 1956), 45.

2. A. Nygren in *Agape and Eros,* trans. P. S. Watson (London: SPCK, 1957), puts forward a powerful statement of this view.

3. This appears to be an unresolved difficulty in E. Thurneysen's account of the relationship between the Word of God and the words of man. See *A Theology of Pastoral Care* (Richmond: John Knox Press, 1962).

4. See Abraham H. Maslow, *Motivation and Personality* (New York: Harper & Brothers, 1954).

5. For a full development of this point see Reinhold Niebuhr, *Moral Man and Immoral Society* (New York: Charles Scribner's Sons, 1932); and see A. Fierro Bardaji, *The Militant Gospel* (Maryknoll, N.Y.: Orbis Books, 1977) for a useful critical survey of recent political theologies.

6. Tillich's shortest exposition of the various forms of love will be found in his *Love, Power and Justice* (New York: Oxford Univ. Press, 1954), chap. 2.

7. The nonsexist term "clergyperson" does not apply to this historical period, in which only men could enter the priesthood.

8. A. M. Carr Saunders and P. A. Wilson, *The Professions* (Oxford: University Press, 1933) provide the standard account of this approach.

9. This is indeed the case, since, for example, journalists, funeral directors, law enforcement officers, and insurance agents are all claiming to belong to professions, on the grounds of lengthy training, disciplinary procedures, and adherence to a service ethic rather than the profit motive.

10. The classical source of the functionalist approach is Everett C. Hughes, *Men and Their Work* (Glencoe, Ill.: Free Press, 1958).

11. P. Wilding, *Professional Power and Social Welfare* (London: Routledge & Kegan Paul, 1982), 5. See also E. Freidson, *Profession of Medicine* (New York: Dodd, Mead & Co., 1970) and T. J. Johnson, *Professions and Power* (London: Macmillan & Co., 1972) for influential accounts of the power struggle approach.

CHAPTER 2

1. Gustaf Wingren, *Luther on Vocation* (Edinburgh: Oliver & Boyd, 1958), 9.

2. Ibid., 43.

3. See Dietrich Bonhoeffer, *Ethics* (London: SCM Press, 1955), 222–30.

4. A good example of this kind of functional definition can be found in a recently published ecumenical statement on ministry: "In order to fullfil its mission the Church needs persons who are publicly and continually responsible for pointing to its fundamental dependence on Jesus Christ, and thereby provide, within a multiplicity of gifts, a focus of its unity," World Council of Churches, *Baptism, Eucharist and Ministry*, Faith and Order Paper III (Geneva: World Council of Churches, 1982), 21.

5. Hans Küng, *Why Priests?* (London: William Collins & Co., 1977), 19.

6. Anthony Russell, *The Clerical Profession* (London: SPCK, 1980), 15.

7. P. Halmos, *The Personal Service Society* (London: Constable, 1970).

8. See H. A. Eadie, "The Helping Personality," *Contact* 49, (Summer 1975): 2–17.

9. The description comes from Lord Chesterfield. See Russell, *Clerical Profession*, 32.

10. Ibid., 22.

11. M. Young, *The Rise of the Meritocracy 1870–2033* (London: Thames & Hudson, 1958).

12. This statement would certainly be questioned by some commentators on modern developments in the Church of England. For example, R. Towler and A. P. M. Coxon have pointed out in *The Fate of the Anglican Clergy* (London: Macmillan & Co., 1979) that there is a drop in educational standards, with an increasing proportion of late entrants and entrants to the nonstipendiary ministry who have a shorter training for the same occupation. The authors take this as one piece of evidence for what they call the "marginalization" of the Anglican clergy.

13. See J. Sanford, *Ministry Burnout* (New York: Paulist Press, 1982).

14. See S. W. Blizzard, "The Minister's Dilemma," *The Christian Century* (25 April 1956): 508–10.

15. J. D. Glasse, *Profession: Minister* (Nashville: Abingdon, 1968), 75–76. For a longer list of "role sectors," viewed from a historical perspective, see Russell, *Clerical Profession*, 7.

16. Towler and Coxon, *Fate of the Anglican Clergy.*

17. Russell, *Clerical Profession,* 305.

18. Towler and Coxon, *Fate of the Anglican Clergy,* 51. Cf. P. Jarvis, "The Ministry: Occupation, Profession or Status?" *Expository Times* 86 (June 1975): 264–67.

19. Thomas C. Oden, *Pastoral Theology* (San Francisco: Harper & Row, 1983), 314.

20. Ibid., 55 and passim.

21. Ibid., 11.

22. Küng, *Why Priests?* 36ff.

23. J. D. G. Dunn, *Unity and Diversity in the New Testament* (London: SCM Press, 1977), 121.

24. Ibid., 122.

25. For a good exposition of these themes see Jürgen Moltmann, *The Church in the Power of the Spirit* (London: SCM Press 1977), 307ff.

CHAPTER 3

1. Quoted by Howard J. Clinebell in "The Challenge of the Speciality of Pastoral Counseling," *Pastoral Psychology* 15 (April 1964): 21.

2. Ibid.

3. The final outcome of this debate was the formation of the Association of Pastoral Care and Counseling (UK), but the character of that organization is very different from the original proposals. It is in effect a federation of various pastoral organizations which does not attempt to regulate, standardize, or otherwise control what happens in the numerous contexts within which pastoral care and counseling is practiced.

4. This was subsequently published in *Contact* (Journal of the Scottish Pastoral Association, the Clinical Theology Association, and the Institute of Religion and Medicine) 35 (June 1971): 24–31.

5. *Contact* 35 (June 1971): 25.

6. Ibid., 27.

7. *Contact* 36 (November 1971): 26–29.

8. Ibid., 27.

9. Alastair Campbell, *Rediscovering Pastoral Care* (Philadelphia: Westminster Press, 1981), 10f., 61f.

10. T. J. Johnson, *Professions and Power* (London: Macmillan & Co.; 1972), chap. 4.

11. See my book *Professional Care: Its Meaning and Practice* (Philadelphia: Fortress Press, 1984) for a more detailed discussion of this problem. See also J. H. Galper, *The Politics of Social Services* (Englewood Cliffs, N.J.: Prentice-Hall, 1975).

12. Don S. Browning, *The Moral Context of Pastoral Care* (Philadelphia: Westminster Press, 1976).

13. "With Love to the U.S.A.," in *Religion and Medicine,* ed. M. A. H. Melinsky (London: SCM Press, 1970), 132–46.

14. Howard J. Clinebell has also been alert to this problem and has explored it in a number of writings, e.g., *Growth Groups* (Nashville: Abingdon Press, 1977) and *Growth Counseling* (Nashville: Abingdon Press, 1979).

15. R. Titmuss, *Commitment to Welfare* (London: George Allen & Unwin, 1968), 85.

CHAPTER 4

1. Since the novel is based on real life the identity of the fictional Dr. Fried ("Furii") can be guessed at as Frieda Fromm-Reichman.

2. T. S. Eliot, *Collected Poems 1909–1962* (London: Faber & Faber, 1963), 63.

3. Dietrich Bonhoeffer, *The Cost of Discipleship* (London: SCM Press, 1948).

4. See, for example, the Code for Nurses published by the International Council of Nurses (Geneva: ICN, 1975).

5. Seward Hiltner's ground-breaking work on pastoral counseling established this point so firmly that, whatever subsequent refinements and modifications have been made to it, it has remained an axiom for virtually all subsequent approaches to pastoral counseling.

6. T. C. Oden's work *Kerygma and Counseling* reprint, San Francisco: Harper & Row, 1978) began to uncover this issue and his *Psychotherapy and Contemporary Theology* (Philadelphia: Westminster Press, 1967) developed it well. See also Don S. Browning, *Atonement and Psychotherapy* (Philadelphia: Westminster Press, 1966).

7. See Susan Sontag, *Illness as Metaphor* (London: Allen Lane, 1979).

8. I have explored this point at greater length in *Rediscovering Pastoral Care* (Philadelphia: Westminster Press, 1981), chap. 5.

CHAPTER 5

1. I have discussed this question elsewhere. See my *Professional Care: Its Meaning and Practice* (Philadelphia: Fortress Press, 1984), chap. 6.

2. Some might question the word "unambiguously" in view of the doctrine of the virgin birth. Yet, whatever the significance of this strand in the tradition, orthodox Christian belief has always stressed the full humanity of Jesus.

3. See J. Bowlby, *Loss: Sadness and Depression,* Attachment and Loss Series, vol. 3 (New York: Basic Books, 1980).

4. P. Selby, *Liberating God: Private Care and Public Struggle* (London: SPCK, 1983), 52.

5. Ibid., 99.

6. See chap. 3 above.

7. T. Kinsella, "The Dispossessed," *Poems 1956–1973* (Winston-Salem, N.C.: Wake Forest Univ. Press, 1980).

CHAPTER 6

1. Martin D'Arcy, *The Mind and Heart of Love* (London: William Collins Sons, 1962), 98.

2. H. Richard Niebuhr, *The Purpose of the Church and Its Ministry* (New York: Harper & Brothers, 1956), 35.

3. William Blake, "The Garden of Love," in *A Choice of Blake's Verse* (London: Faber & Faber, 1970.)

Select Bibliography

Glasse, J. D. *Profession: Minister.* Nashville: Abingdon Press, 1964. Argues the case for regarding the ministry as a profession.

Holifield, E. B. *A History of Pastoral Care in America: From Salvation to Self Realization.* Nashville: Abingdon Press, 1983.

Johnson, T.J. *Professions and Power.* London: Macmillan & Co., 1972. A clear summary of sociological theories of professionalization.

Küng, Hans. *Why Priests?* London: William Collins & Co., 1977. Radical questioning of clericalism, with good historical background.

Moltmann, Jürgen. *The Church in the Power of the Spirit.* London: SCM Press, 1977. Theological background to the ministry of the whole church.

Oden, Thomas C. *Pastoral Theology: Essentials of Ministry.* San Francisco: Harper & Row, 1983. Argues for a return to the centrality of the ordained ministry in pastoral theology and pastoral practice.

Russell, Anthony. *The Clerical Profession.* London: SPCK, 1980. A richly documented historical account of clerical developments in the Church of England, which is of interest in relation to Holifield's *History of Pastoral Care in America* (see above).

Stewart, C. W. *Person and Profession: Career Development in the Ministry.* Nashville: Abingdon Press, 1974. Deals with a range of practical problems arising from changing roles of ministers.

Wilding, P. *Professional Power and Social Welfare.* London: Routledge & Kegan Paul, 1982. Reveals the moral ambiguities of professional care.

Wingren, G. *The Christian's Calling: Luther on Vocation.* Edinburgh: Oliver & Boyd, 1958. A valuable source of information on Luther's emphasis on the vocation of all Christians.

World Council of Churches. *Baptism, Eucharist and Ministry.* Faith and Order Paper 111. Geneva: World Council of Churches, 1982. An ecumenical statement on ministry prepared jointly by WCC representatives and representatives of the Roman Catholic Church.

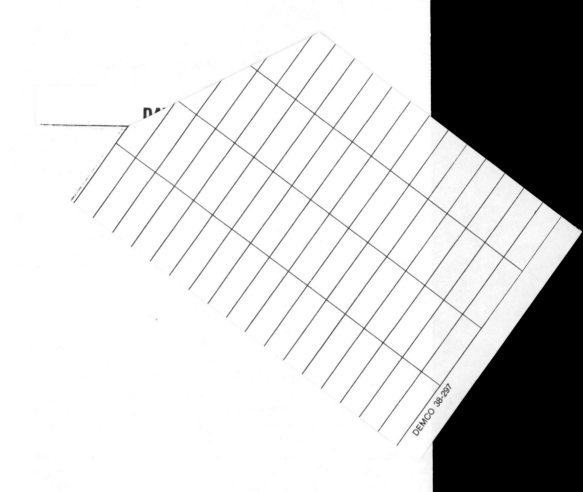

DEMCO 38-297